HISTORY IN CRISIS?

Recent Directions in Historiography

Third Edition

Norman J. Wilson
Messiah College

Boston Columbus Indianapolis New York San Francisco Upper Saddle River
Amsterdam Cape Town Dubai London Madrid Milan Munich Paris Montréal Toronto
Delhi Mexico City São Paulo Sydney Hong Kong Seoul Singapore Taipei Tokyo

Editor in Chief: Ashley Dodge
Editorial Assistant: Nicole Suddeth
Director of Marketing: Brandy Dawson
Executive Marketing Manager: Kelly May
Senior Marketing Coordinator:
 Theresa Rotondo
Managing Editor: Denise Forlow
Program Manager: Kathy Sleys
Senior Operations Supervisor: Mary Fischer
Operations Specialist: Mary Ann Gloriande
Art Director: Jayne Conte
Cover Designer: Suzanne Duda

Cover Image: Fine Art Images /
 SuperStock
Director of Digital Media: Brian Hyland
Digital Media Editor: Rachel Comerford
Digital Media Project Manager:
 Tina Gagliostro
**Full-Service Project Management and
 Composition:** Murugesh Rajkumar
 Namasivayam/PreMediaGlobal
Printer/Binder/Cover Printer:
 Courier Companies
Text Font: Palatino LT Std 10.5/12

Credits and acknowledgments borrowed from other sources and reproduced, with permission, in this textbook appear on appropriate page within text.

Library of Congress Cataloging-in-Publication Data

Wilson, Norman James, 1958-
 History in crisis? : Recent directions in historiography / Norman J. Wilson,
 Messiah College.—Third edition.
 pages cm
 Includes bibliographical references and index.
 ISBN-13: 978-0-205-84895-9 (alk. paper)
 ISBN-10: 0-205-84895-8 (alk. paper)
1. Historiography. 2. History—Philosophy. 3. History—Methodology. I. Title.
 D13.W59 2013
 907.2—dc23

2013008561

ISBN 10: 0-205-84895-8
ISBN 13: 978-0-205-84895-9

36 2022

To my wife Tarja
and our sons
James, Christopher, and David

Contents

Preface

"The historical ignorance of the average high school and undergraduate student is nothing short of appalling. For many of them rulers, wars, legislation, influential people, and inventions swirl disconnected in an unstructured, chaotic past. Few possess any meaningful chronological or geographical frameworks to help them organize disparate bits and pieces of historical information. . . . What is most depressing is that so many are content to remain ignorant of history. The past, except in specific areas such as rock music, pop culture, and sports, is simply not important enough to justify let alone motivate them to become better educated."

(Donald A. Yerxa, "Introduction: Historians' Audiences" section of his book.
Recent Themes on Historians and the Public: Historians in Conversation, Columbia,
South Carolina: University of South Carolina Press, 2009, p. 1)

History is both what happened in the past (as real as the global earth) and the stories that one tells about that past (as real as the flat earth was to those who told that story). These histories, or stories, about the past include some things and exclude others. This does not mean that history books are fictional, or made up, stories of the past. It simply means that the writing of history involves choices that allow the past to be told in a shortened, and thus distorted, version.

Students learn the facts, theories, and stories that their culture has determined to be necessary for a proper education. As college curricula have shifted from required courses in the history of the United States or in Western civilization courses to required courses in world civilizations, students have been asked to become familiar with wider histories. One side effect of requiring a wider breadth of knowledge is that students may not know traditional, regional, or national history as well as students in the recent past. This has allowed critics to condemn students for their lack of historical knowledge.

The students that Yerxa condemns in the opening quotation are not opposed to the field of history, they simply prefer a history that they view as relevant. Historians could cater to the tastes of students and write histories of rock music, pop culture, and sports. Or historians can take the topics that they believe to be important and present them in a manner that students find relevant. Historians need to consider not just the content of their stories, but also the manner in which they tell those stories. It is easy to blame the youth of America, as Yerxa does, and far more difficult to convey one's story in a manner that young people around the world find interesting and engaging.

The first edition of this book was motivated by a desire to make historiography, or the history of the writing of history, relevant to students. The act of writing a book changes the ideas of the author as the book that one sets out to write is rarely the same as the final project. Perhaps the most revealing aspect of the third edition of this book is my own recognition that my notions of history have evolved over the 15 years that I have worked on the various editions. Years ago I remember my adamant support that college history students were involved in an exercise of explaining causal changes over time. Some students complained that their high school teachers had a notion of history that involved factual knowledge that one needed to know in order to be successful. I wanted students not only to move beyond the wall of facts notion of history, but also to embrace history as a story of what caused things to change over time. My understanding of the importance of causal history has changed since writing the first edition.

Recently, one student in my "World Civilization" course came to my office in distress because she was having trouble reading the textbook. She reported that the book was overwhelming and she could not figure out which names and concepts were the most significant. Specifically, she wanted 15–20 terms per chapter that she could define and know. I showed her that the syllabus explained clearly that she was to write sweeping essays on one of four topics. The topics themselves defined which terms were important. If she wanted to focus on politics then she should know the names of rulers and political theorists, but if she wanted to focus on cultural history then she would need to mine a different set of names and ideas from the reading. The course would weave the four themes together into a tapestry about causal change. My attempts to explain that history is more than a wall of facts fell on deaf ears. She knew what history was and she needed those terms. I explained that causal arguments needed to be based on historical facts, but that the scope of what was a significant fact was also contingent on the causal argument one wanted to craft. My explanation was of little comfort. She dropped my course and took one from a colleague who provided lists of important terms in the syllabus. The other instructor expected her to memorize definitions and regurgitate facts on fill-in-the-blank examinations.

I have shifted away from my adamant support of essays full of causal change over time, but I have done so without reverting to the wall-of-facts theory of history that allowed my former colleague to offer fill-in-the-blank examinations. He is not entirely to blame, as his own mentor was famous for sending graduate students to the archive to fill in a gap in the professional wall of knowledge. The old stone wall of facts that defined the field had some weak stones in a few places and if the new graduate students would simply go to the archive and fill in the gaps, we could refortify the field of history. My mentor was equally interested in archival work, but he wanted us to bring a strong familiarity with theory into the archives. Rather than repairing the decaying wall of facts, we were encouraged to reconsider the theories of the field and of related fields.

New theories will force historians to look at the past anew. Recent developments in theory have forced me to reassess my own focus on causal change over time. The shift away from pure causal change over time frees historians from a timeline unfolding of history whereby X caused Y and now we have Z (what is defined below as a diachronic unfolding of history). Change occurs over time, but not always in the neat and precise unfolding that is the focus of causal history. The "literary turn," the "cultural turn," and the rise of a new intellectual history that explored things occurring at the same time in a wide range of fields (synchronic instead of diachronic history) were three factors instrumental in the shift of focus of histories from the chronological unfolding of change toward explanations that highlighted the diversity and messiness of the past. The scope of history was shifting at the same time that the new global curriculum was forcing a reassessment of other theoretical and methodological issues.

One goal of this book is to describe a variety of methodological issues not so that students will be amazed by the diversity, but rather so that they can understand the advantages and limitations of the predominant world view of their culture. This will allow historians to create useful stories of the past that are viewed as valid by the widest audience possible. Historians have long grappled with the breadth of their audience: Should they write for other professional historians, for students of history, or for a general public? With the growth of world civilization courses, historians have been forced to move beyond traditional national (U.S. survey courses) and even regional (Western civilization courses) frameworks. World civilization courses have forced historians to reassess the scope, themes, and schools of history.

Accepted practices for writing history have changed in the 15 years that have passed since I wrote the first edition of this book. Critics may claim that some of the new theories and practices are ruining history, but I contend that the changes bring exciting opportunities. The very fact that historiographical orthodoxy is changing over time may be the best evidence that history is not in crisis. The diverse theories and practices described in this book may appear daunting to students of history, but their very existence is evidence of the vitality of history as a field of study. Students of history need to be familiar not only with specific areas of content, but also with current theories and practices. In an effort to keep students abreast of recent developments in the field, this third edition includes several significant changes.

NEW TO THIS EDITION

- Exploration of new theories such as tricontinentalism
- Examination of how postmodernism has forced scholars to reassess modernism, modernization, and modernity
- Discussion of whether there is progress in history and/or progress in historical methodology
- Digital history
- New or revised sections on structuralism, semiotics, and poststructuralism
- Updates on intellectual history, the cultural turn, and postcolonialism

This text is available in a variety of formats—digital and print. To learn more about our programs, pricing options, and customization, visit www.pearsonhighered.com.

ACKNOWLEDGMENTS

I would like to thank my current and former students and colleagues at Messiah College and Methodist University for their support and encouragement. I have learned more from them than they have from me. I would also like to thank the Pearson reviewers of this edition and of previous editions for their helpful comments: Wynn Gadkar-Wilcox, *Western Connecticut State University*; Jurgen Buchenau, *UNC Charlotte*; Charles Connell, *Northern Arizona University*; Daniel Vivian, *University of Louisville*; Donal O'Sullivan, *California State University Northridge*; Daniel Schafer, *Belmont University*; Christopher Snyder, *Marymount University*; Georg G. Iggers, *SUNY Buffalo*; Matt K. Matsuda, *Rutgers University*; and Clarke Garrett, *Dickinson College*.

Chapter 1

What Was History?

History is both a subject, or what has happened, and the process of recounting and analyzing that subject. Because history is "what happened," there is a tendency to view it as a collection of facts. These "facts" are supposedly derived from a single body of evidence. Students frequently assume that history is "objective," meaning that any individual observing the evidence will come to the same conclusion. If so, historical facts would be similar to scientific facts deduced from observation and experimentation. A scientist can read about a new fact and then repeat an experiment and come to the same conclusion. The nature of historical evidence is actually quite distinct from scientific evidence because history cannot be repeated in similar conditions. Historical "facts" are what the historian happens, or chooses, to find. These facts may change once the historian learns more about the topic. Historians strive to be as objective, or unbiased, as possible, but the inability to repeat an experiment means that historical analysis is not as objective as scientific analysis. The act of recounting what has happened introduces a degree of ambiguity into history because different perspectives of what happened create different histories. Historical facts therefore are unlike scientific facts that can be re-verified when needed.

In history, the answers that one "finds" are contingent on the extant fragments from the past and the questions that one poses about those fragments. Historical questions assert a strong directive influence on historical inquiry, but the very existence of historical records, or traces of the past, is directive as well. Traces of the past exist before the historical inquiry, and they become the material of directive inquiry. When writing history, historians pose questions and search the existing historical remnants. The remnants force historians to revise their theories just as the theories constantly modify the way that one understands the evidence. Historical evidence and hypotheses constantly modify each other in a process of dialectical feedback. Historians usually have more evidence to deal with than they can use. So historians filter out a good deal of evidence in a process of subjective choice where the "facts" they "find" are either consciously or subconsciously selected. When one adds the problem of evidence that disappears, crucial facts that never were recorded, and documents that were destroyed, the obvious conclusion is that the historical record is incomplete.

How do historians actually practice history in such an environment? Take the example of coming home and finding that your roommate's things have been removed from your apartment. Because you are a history major (as is the absent roommate), you confidently begin to reconstruct what has happened based on the remnants that remain. Your historical analysis follows a basic three-stage process of (1) gathering evidence, (2) analyzing the evidence in order to establish facts, and (3) drawing conclusions from the facts. You have thus moved objectively from observable evidence to hard facts and rational conclusions.

But is that really what you or most historians would do? After searching briefly through the apartment for any sign of your roommate, would you not jump to conclusions and develop a theory that you attempt to prove? For instance, the telephone bill must have arrived, and your roommate finally had to face the reality of having a lover who lives thousands of miles away. Or perhaps the results of a recent history exam forced your roommate to realize that the semester on academic probation will actually be the last semester in college. You search frantically through the mail for a copy of the telephone bill, or you call a friend who is enrolled in your roommate's history class. You pose a series of theories and try to prove each one. Over the course of the next few days, you truly are convinced at various times that you know the correct theory and you go to great lengths to substantiate each theory.

Earlier we said that history consists of (1) what happened and (2) the process of recounting it. Your roommate disappeared, and over the next few days, you proceed to recount what happened to various people. You construct many histories of what happened. Even if your roommate called and explained the "truth" about the sudden disappearance, your explanation would change as you shifted the blame from yourself to the rigors of academic life to the exorbitant cost of higher education. Each time you retell what happened your explanation varies slightly.

Historians formulate a problem that seems interesting—a hypothesis, if you will—and then they look for evidence. The historical evidence will not always fit the original hypothesis, and thus the historian modifies the hypothesis. The result is a process of dialectical feedback in which evidence and hypothesis constantly modify each other. Historians tend to discard evidence that seems irrelevant to their purposes even though other historians might consider that evidence to be of vital importance. Other evidence may force the historian to revise an argument. In the end, historians never seem to write the book they set out to write.

"History" is best defined as a continual, open-ended process of argument. No question is closed because any problem can be reopened by finding new evidence or by taking a new look at old evidence. Thus there are no final answers, only good, coherent arguments: history is not some irreducible list of "the facts" but continually changing bodies of evidence.

The historical account of Christopher Columbus, the Renaissance explorer who sailed the ocean blue, offers an example of how historical perspectives change as a result of (1) different political agendas, (2) different cultural assumptions, (3) different historical methodology, and (4) different focuses of study. The discovery of new Columbus material between 1892 and 1992 played virtually no role in a one-hundred-year transformation of the historical account of Christopher Columbus. In 1892, the four-hundredth anniversary of Columbus's 1492 voyage, celebrations took place on both sides of the Atlantic Ocean. These Europe-centered commemorations praised the triumphant European civilization and celebrated the spread of Christianity to savages. Frederick Jackson Turner used the Columbian Exposition as an opportunity to explain all American development in terms of his "frontier thesis."[1] Turner's thesis was printed in the *Annual Report of the American Historical Association for the Year 1893*. Of course a few voices in 1892 recognized some regrettable misunderstandings, but basically the first voyage of Columbus was viewed as one part of a great scheme of progress from which all benefited.

By 1992, the historical accounts of Columbus's "discoveries" differed markedly from the 1882 depictions in spite of the fact that few "new" facts about Columbus had been discovered. Instead, the new perspective was a product of new political agendas, cultural assumptions, historical methodologies, and historical focal points. Decolonization raised issues about the validity of Eurocentric triumphalism because colonized peoples drew attention to the price they had been forced to pay. Cultural assumptions about historical progress ceased to be tenable in light of two world wars, the Holocaust, atomic and nuclear weapons, and the Gulags. Certainly, assumptions about historical progress itself appeared less credible. In addition, new understanding of ecology, disease, and economics radically altered historians' assessments of the impact of discoveries on the "New World." Historians also adopted methodologies from related fields such as anthropology, sociology, and psychology. Historical methods themselves changed in part because the rise of mass political parties challenged the idea that one heroic individual changed history. Twentieth-century changes created a different framework for interpreting the past and thereby destroyed the Eurocentric 1892 view.

The ensuing freedom from master narratives, like the 1882 histories of Columbus, grants historians a degree of creative freedom. This creative freedom runs the risk of becoming a free-for-all that reduces history to fiction. The literary aspect of writing history obviously involves some biases, but this fact does not mean that we cannot understand a text or an event within its historical context. The apparent relativism of Columbus interpretation does not mean that all viewpoints are equally valid. Historical questions have enormous directive power in historical inquiry, but traces of the past existed before simple curiosity brought historians to them. Regardless of the subjectivity of historians, the past is a once-existent reality. It is this quality of the past that makes it uniquely compelling and distinct from fiction. Perhaps a rampant historical bias will produce a fiction, but historically the community of scholars will disregard it as such. Historians create Archimedean points from which they make value judgments about the past. Historians therefore monitor themselves and maintain standards for acceptable history that will be dealt with later in this text.

This text is based on the assumption that historians can protect history from the purported crisis by pursuing six reasons for studying history:

1. *Change*: History can cure us of provincialism by showing that change is one constant of the human experience.

2. *Time*: Time is of great significance to historical change because it is irreversible. Time is to history what space is to anthropology. History highlights differences over periods of time, and anthropology distinguishes differences between various places with greater emphasis on spatial variations than historical variations. Experiments in science can change by replacing one thing with another, whereas history is unrepeatable; once something has happened, it cannot be replicated because knowledge about what has happened changes what might happen in the future. History then is a natural process that is irreversible. This process, according to French sociologist Pierre Bourdieu, involves the creation of "habitus," which simply means that historical changes make certain behavior commonplace and unreflective.

3. *Otherness*: The result of change over time is that the past is radically different from the present and the future. This is a defining feature of the modern view of history in which historians reveal the foreignness of the past. History reveals the foreignness of the past and anthropology the foreignness of others in the present. This view constitutes a clear break from previous conceptions of history such as the Enlightenment notions of David Hume and Edward Gibbon. Depicting the past as a foreign land and revealing the evolution to the present, such as Norbert Elias's delineation of the evolution of polite manners, reveals

the contingency of our own circumstances. Change over time means that humans may be different in the future. If the past was the same as the present, then there would be little reason to study history; namely, the present with its abundance of sources would offer more fruitful study than the past. Historians differ from most social scientists on precisely this point: the otherness of the past means that change over time should be the focal point of understanding why things are the way they are. Historians therefore explain how we got from the past to the present.

    4. *Perspective*: The realization of otherness makes us open to other perspectives. History reveals the uncanniness of our world and our own past by taking topics that are important and showing how historically conditioned our own situation is. Perspective shows why respective subjects are worthy of historical importance. Perspective demonstrates how something that otherwise strikes us as natural, given, and inherent was in fact created in history. Perspective cures us of our provincialism by revealing the extent to which our current existence is both contingent and ephemeral.

    5. *Collective memory*: History is to society what memory is to an individual. Our collective memory of the past allows us to understand ourselves as part of a society formed through time. The necessity of memory is obvious, but can we have too much of a good thing? Can we have too much history like the Luggnaggians in Jonathan Swift's *Gulliver's Travels*? Friedrich Nietzsche warned in *The Advantage and Disadvantage of History for Life* that memory and action contradict each other, and thus the danger of too much memory would be a culture that cannot act. So historians need to craft a collective memory that reveals our past without burdening us with it.

    6. *Ambition*: Ambitious historians will be able to create a collective memory that does not overburden us. Lack of ambition is one of the occupational hazards of a discipline whose cardinal rule is sticking to the facts. Ambitious historians may sacrifice completeness or consistency, but if powerfully motivated, they create new ways of constructing our collective memory. Political and ideological commitments create passionate historians and provide new questions and answers. Ambitious historians provide students of history new ways of imagining the past, present, and future.

1.1   HISTORICAL TIME AND TELEOLOGY

What is time? When asked, "What time is it?" the average person responds without hesitation, whereas a slight change in the wording to "What is time?" frequently produces long pauses. We take time for granted and all too often assume that all people conceive of time as linear and noncyclical. Most ancient cultures conceived of time as a cyclical, three-dimensional thing to which they attached little importance. Time was often depicted as a snake eating its own tail. The choice of a snake is revealing because as the snake sheds its skin it appears to become younger again. Time, like the shedding of a snake's skin, repeated itself and was therefore given less importance. Classical conceptions of time were more complex than this description, but the simple point remains that linear notions of time are not universal.

The contemporary notion of time is linear and two-dimensional: we remember the past but live truly in the present without claiming to know the future. Other conceptions of time include a three-dimensional one that views time much as we view space. For instance, contemporary Hmong culture believes that the past coexists with the present and has an obvious influence both on the present and on the future.[2] In this view, the past played a major part in the present because the present fates were predestined.

Most Western thinkers have rejected cyclical concepts of time. Sir Isaac Newton actually separated time from the universe. If time and the universe are separate, then can either exist without the other? Immanuel Kant argued that time cannot exist without the universe because it is impossible to conceive of a timeless universe (this was necessary for Sir Isaac Newton). The problem derives from theories of the origin of the universe. If the universe was created, then time is not independent of the universe because time and the universe were presumably created together. Albert Einstein, on the other hand, connected time to the universe without recourse to any theory of creation. The point of mentioning these changing theories of time is to encourage a reconsideration of our conceptualization of time and its implications for the writing of history.

One danger of championing a linear, two-dimensional view of history is the classic historical fallacy of teleology. Teleology involves uncovering great developmental patterns in history that show either progress or decline. A famous example of teleological historical writing is the Whiggish pursuit of history moving toward a goal. "Whig history," broadly defined, is a school of English historians, the best known being Thomas Babington Macaulay, who believed in the culmination of historical development because they saw themselves as the apex of historical development. Herbert Butterfield coined the term "Whig history" as a derogatory label for the moralistic and pragmatic tendencies he criticized in his 1931 book *The Whig Interpretation of History*. More narrowly defined, the term refers to (1) a study of the past with reference to the present, (2) a pursuit of causal agency in history based on the assumption that God was the original cause, and (3) a generational delineation of "a clash of wills out of which there emerges something that probably no man ever willed" but that the Whig historian is able to make intelligible to the present. This nineteenth-century English school of writing was interested in parliamentary institutions. Whig historians studied the evolution of government because they were reformers with a passion for civil liberties.

The Whig concept of development-over-time made the comprehension of history a crucial prerequisite to understanding the present and preparing for the future. The past mattered, in a way that was neither random nor cyclical. The notion of "development over time" can aim at a known, acknowledged goal, such as the Judeo-Christian notions of a Messiah or Second Coming, or it may avoid any set future because we do not know where the future is heading. The developmental unfolding of time, be it toward a future goal or simply from the past to the present, is known as teleology.

Teleology, the uncovering of great developmental patterns in history, is inherent to the study of history because historians know what happened in the past. The path to the present frequently appears predetermined and inevitable because we look at the past in retrospect, know the outcome, and trace what happened. For instance, historians have evidence that was unavailable to contemporaries of the bombing of Pearl Harbor and thus speculate about why Americans did not see what was about to happen. Evidence and perspective allow historians to imagine possible alternatives. When we scoff at Neville Chamberlain getting off the plane on the eve of World War II and saying "peace for our time," we are scoffing at a lack of vision. The act of appeasing Hitler and the failure to recognize the impending attack on Pearl Harbor offer many avenues for historical evaluation not so that we can write interesting fiction novels, but rather in order to sharpen our vision about how we should act. How will historians view us in sixty years? Do we currently perceive factors significant to the future, or will later historians find evidence that we missed? How do we ascertain the direction in which we are headed? What if we, like Chamberlain, are wrong? Do current moves toward world peace, free trade, and good international relations contain the seeds of destruction, or are we on the road to geopolitical nirvana?

Teleology frequently results in a history of the winners without adequate consideration of other outcomes that might have occurred. For instance, modernization theorists such as the economic historian Walt W. Rostow pose a theory of industrialized nations whereby all nations that modernize will follow the pattern that other (modernized) nations have followed. Alexander Gerschenkron tempers the notion of modernization teleology by arguing that some nations industrialize first and later nations follow different patterns because they need to compete with existing industrialized countries. Another popular paradigm, influenced by the French tradition of socioeconomic history, is found in Immanuel Wallerstein's neo-Marxist analysis of development: *The Modern World-System* (1974).[3] Wallerstein defines Western Europe as the core of development and then examines its interaction with what he terms the "periphery" and "semiperiphery." Rostow, Gerschenkron, and Wallerstein all pose theories of development that are teleological.

Teleology cannot be avoided, but it can be curtailed to tolerable levels by resisting the temptation to find a goal toward which history supposedly is moving. One way to avoid overly teleological history is to consider how things could have happened differently.

Edward Shorter, an excellent historian who was also involved in the late 1960s' counterculture movement, wrote a titillating article in 1972 about sexuality and social change in Europe.[4] At the height of the "sexual revolution," Shorter wrote about sexual patterns of the past, but with a teleological bent that placed himself as the pinnacle of history and thus the outcome of historical development. The metaphorical side of his article had clear contemporary connotations: it was also part of a larger political goal of late 1960s' counterculture in that Shorter tried to persuade the American working class to support the students in their protest. Shorter's political agenda was very transparent, and his theory has not stood the test of time: in the age of AIDS we have a new perspective for evaluating the "sexual revolution"—safe sex has replaced free sex. Shorter's optimistic history of progress could thus be rejected in favor of a theory of decline. But that would simply replace the teleology of progress with the teleology of decline. Contemporary historians of sexual practices tend to consider how things could have happened differently, thereby rejecting Shorter's teleology without succumbing to a pessimistic teleology of further decline.

Teleology cannot be completely avoided because we will always interpret the past from a perspective of contemporary knowledge. This perspective is one of the reasons that teleology is so attractive to historians. After all, most historians attempt to clarify the past by making it logical and comprehensible. What use is a history that muddles the past? The tendency to tidy up the past from the perspective of the present allows historians to champion their own values by placing them in a position of understanding instead of confusion. The teleological problem becomes a quantitative conundrum: what degree of teleology is tolerable?

1.2 A BRIEF HISTORY OF HISTORY

Western history was initially a disadvantaged discipline because cyclical notions of history meant that early peoples attached little importance to time. For instance, Homer's *Iliad* is not a history of the Trojan War so much as an account of the dramatic high points with a fictional emphasis on the gods' intervention. The work is highly moralistic and offers mythical explanations based on divine action. Later Greek historians, notably Hecataeus of Miletus and Herodotus in the fifth century BC, began to emphasize distinctly rational explanations. The two sought rational ways to explain why the Greeks and Persians fought based on the customs and values of the two peoples. Their histories maintained a moralistic perspective but displayed a new sense of morality concerned with what motivates humans to take action. Thucydides's analysis of the Peloponnesian War later that same century is a coldly realistic study of the pursuit of power that emphasizes the need to understand the complexity of human motivations. The work assumes that humans have a set nature; hence, the potential exists for understanding the future actions of humans by studying what they have done in the past.

Despite the markedly higher standards for historical analysis of the fifth century BC, the writing of history remained a disadvantaged discipline in ancient Greece. In fact, Aristotle introduced a hierarchical distinction between history, poetry, and philosophy whereby history was the inferior form of knowledge. He viewed history as the study of individuals and their lone reactions; hence, history focused on the particular, whereas poetry and philosophy dealt with universals. Aristotle's distinction between universals and the particular survived long after Western conceptions of time evolved into a decidedly linear notion.

The Judeo-Christian notion of God revealed through linear time provided history a different role in religion: historical progression became evidence of divine design and direction. The Jewish notion of a covenant with God created a new sense of history. Because Jews have an obligation to uphold the covenant, they need to understand the past, or the terms of the covenant, in order to know how to act in the future. History has importance because they are looking forward to God's promises in a teleological manner. Christianity is almost completely a religion of historians: it is catechistic, meaning that believers must accept the truth of Christian history (the catechism); it is linear instead of cyclical, as shown by the BC and AD form of dating based on time before and after Jesus; and it is teleological with a clear beginning, a central event, and a theory about where history is heading in the future.

St Augustine, in *The City of God*, codified a Christian tradition of history that is (1) teleological, a product of divine creation with an ultimate goal at the end of a linear progression; (2) rational, directed by the logic of God's law and providence; and (3) tragic, in that tragic points of history accentuate human failings and instruct believers to adhere to God's rational plan. This Christian view of history dominated European thought until Renaissance thinkers began to emphasize secular ideals derived from ancient Greek and Roman models. The Renaissance historical method de-emphasized Christian teleology, opting instead to view events within a strong cultural context. Philologists such as Lorenzo Valla studied language within its context in order to reveal the historical meaning of a text. Valla proved, for instance, that the "Donation of Constantine," a document that purportedly gave the Pope secular jurisdiction over the states around Rome, was a forgery. Valla used history and linguistics to prove his case: (1) an historical appreciation of Constantine suggested that Constantine would not voluntarily abdicate land to the pope and, more importantly, (2) Latin words used in the text did not exist in Constantine's era. This combination of historical common sense and irreconcilable language was one of the first attacks on a significant Western European document that had been accepted as true and factual. Valla's approach was similar to those developed a few decades earlier in northern Africa. Ibn Khaldun, a North African legal scholar and historian, constructed a logical methodology for evaluating historical accuracy. One of his many examples involved a historical critique of the Bible and specifically the validity of the book of Numbers. According to Numbers, Moses's army had 600,000 people. Khaldun showed that this figure was not possible: (1) no political organization at that time possessed the logistical ability to maneuver such an army (Persia, the largest political power of the era, had an army of at most 120,000) and (2) the army supposedly consisted solely of descendants of Jacob just four generations after Jacob. Khaldun and Valla proved that tools of historical analysis allow us to know more about something than people knew in the past.

The Renaissance undermining of church texts challenged religious authority in general and began a process that liberated history from theology. Two Renaissance historians, Niccolò Machiavelli and Francesco Guicciardini, expanded history beyond the Judeo-Christian tradition and devalued the Christian notion of teleology. They inherited a teleological, linear view of history and proceeded to mold it into a sense of historical periods with each period varying slightly from others. This sense of period provided a new impetus for the concept of anachronism, which is simply the representation of something that existed or happened at other than its proper or historical time. History as periods with potential anachronisms ceased to be consistent with Christian teleology.

Renaissance mysticism, alchemy, and Neoplatonic notions suggested that the world could be understood via comprehensive keys to nature. The scientific program of the sixteenth and seventeenth centuries built on that assumption and on the quantitative methods of measurement and careful observation that were so prevalent among Renaissance engineers, architects, and artists. For instance, the quantitative astronomers rejected the Aristotelian notions of qualitative science and turned to theoretical statements that could be expressed in quantitative terms. The Polish cleric Nicolaus Copernicus initially placed the sun at the center of the universe in order to rescue circular motion while simplifying the system. Tycho Brahe erroneously placed the earth back at the center of the solar system, but his accurate observations of the stars were combined with a mathematical sophistication that Copernicus lacked. Johannes Kepler used the work of his teacher Brahe to correct

Copernicus's sun-centered, or heliocentric, system. Kepler also developed three laws of motion that are mathematical and verifiable in order to explain the movement of the planets. Galileo's observations with the telescope suggested that the universe was rational and that the physical laws that explain the phenomena in the heavens are equally applicable on earth. Rationality and the logic of mathematics replaced the rather sensible and sophisticated, albeit mistaken, Aristotelian view of the cosmos. Galileo also offered rules of motion that were abstractions but, like Kepler's laws, were applicable everywhere.

The scientific revolution had implications for history because human society could potentially be studied like any natural event. Since science sought to uncover the laws and regularities that governed nature, should not history seek to uncover the regularities and tendencies of humans? History modeled on science was not teleological; historians were exploring regularities without an evolutionary paradigm suggesting that these regularities were headed somewhere. In the eighteenth century, Enlightenment historians returned to Renaissance notions of progress but now within the framework of scientific regularities. The new teleology was based on a profound belief in progress evident in Condorcet's 1793 treatise *The Progress of the Human Mind*:

> The sole foundation for belief in the natural sciences is this idea, that the general laws directing the phenomena of the universe, known or unknown, are necessary and constant. Why should this principle be any less true for the development of the intellectual and moral faculties of man than for the other operations of nature?

Condorcet developed scientific ambitions for history: human society and activities fall under regularities like other natural events, so they can and should be studied like science.

In the nineteenth century, Auguste Comte turned this idea of progress into a three-stage teleological view evolving toward positivism. Nineteenth-century positivists believed that factual knowledge about cause and effect could be obtained by objective analysis of data. *Positivism* was the culmination of Comte's three historical stages: (1) the theological, when all was interpreted in terms of God; (2) the metaphysical, when Christians learned to think abstractly; and (3) the positive, or scientific, when objective and precise understanding became possible.

Comte's English contemporary Henry Thomas Buckle championed the scientific approach to history to such an extreme that he replaced Aristotle's ultimate goals of poetry and philosophy with science. Buckle argued that we must understand the past scientifically. He claimed that humans function according to patterns, instead of following free will. Human patterns and tendencies are frequently mistaken for free will when in fact humans act more like busy ants who work without knowing where they are going. For instance, most married people claim that they married out of choice, that they exercised their free will and got married. But the tendency to marry is so strong that a scientific historian such as Buckle could conclude that free will is a delusion and people marry because society programs them to do so.

Buckle and scientific historians placed science, instead of the Aristotelian goals of poetry and philosophy, at the top of the intellectual hierarchy. Moreover, the teleological notion of history was modified in a nontheological fashion; namely, secular progress occurred in history. History was seen to be moving in a particular direction: things were purportedly getting better because rationality and enlightenment were thought to be increasing. Many historians began to view the study of history as the most important form of human knowledge.

1.3 NINETEENTH-CENTURY HISTORICISM

In the nineteenth century, a further revolution in historical thought involved the assertion that historicism was the best way to approach history. Historicism is the belief that each age is particular to itself and that the goal of history is uncovering this specificity (i.e., Vico's *New Science* and Herder's never-completed *Ideas for a Philosophical History of Mankind*).[5] This focus on the specificity of the past involves rejecting the assumption that science is the real form of knowledge and history is a lower form. In fact, history is seen as equal to, or even greater than, science.

Friedrich Meinecke's two-volume analysis of the origins of historicism, *Die Entstehung des Historismus* (Munich, R. Oldenbourg, 1936), distinguished between universalizing, generalizing, and individualizing. Historicism for him was interested in the individual and sought to put the individual and events into context. Meinecke emphasized the diversity of particular historical forms and the multiplicity of individual manifestations instead of general laws and universal structures. Enlightenment writers had emphasized reason and the rational self over faith and the religious self. Consequently, human existence replaced the Augustinian "City of God" as the focal point of history and human understanding. Historicism combined Enlightenment rationalism with the Romantic critique of that rationalism.

Giambattista Vico argued in the eighteenth century that history is the key to understanding the human world. The natural world does not equal the human-made world, and while we may never be able to understand the natural world we can understand the human world. Vico's *verum-factum* principle (the truth is what is made) means that humans cannot know the laws of the natural world because humans did not make that world. What humans can know is human nature through the study of the history that they do make. Historians then can understand the human world better than scientists can understand the natural world. The individualistic past is thus championed over scientific universals.

Johann Gottfried von Herder offered another historicist perspective whereby we cannot compare the past with the present. Herder rejected the Enlightenment notion of universal human nature and argued instead for the uniqueness of each culture. His experiences as a Prussian living in the Latvian city of Riga, where Lettish was spoken, led him to consider the role of language in cultural development. This approach contributed to his theory that cultures are unique because of the organic development of language, itself the essence of identity. Herder's emphasis on the organic development of unique cultures was at odds with David Hume's Enlightenment claim that in order to understand the French and German cultures, all one had to do was study Roman and Greek cultures. The otherness of cultures meant that events should be examined for their validity in and of themselves. We must look at each age on its own terms instead of comparing the past with the present.

The historicist revenge on Enlightenment ideas culminated in Georg Hegel's championing of history as the ultimate form of knowledge. Truth for Hegel was revealed through the progression of history. Hegel denied the existence of static essences because nothing in the world has not evolved. The absence of static essences means that everything must be understood historically because even sciences evolve historically. History therefore applies to everything including "objective" science. Just as modern scientists can understand scientific truths better than earlier scientists, so too historians can understand truth better than their predecessors. The problem with Hegel's solution is that he maintained a teleological goal whereby the task of historians was to show us where we are headed. So Hegel emphasized historicist ideas but within a teleological framework that nineteenth-century historicists rejected.

The notions of linearity and development are crucial to historical thinking, but the modern conception of history did not start until historicism undercut the teleological notions of the Enlightenment. This breakthrough to modern history began with Leopold von Ranke, a German nationalist historian best known for his adage *wie es eigentlich gewesen* (what actually happened). Ranke denied teleology any role in history and argued that the ultimate goal of history is to understand the past as it really was. His emphasis on understanding the past on its own terms meant that historians would avoid wearing the spectacles of the present as they pursued the individuality and process of history.

The scientific objectivity of Ranke's historicism became the foundation of history in the late nineteenth and early twentieth centuries. This history was (1) hermeneutic, based on documents and textual analysis;

(2) historicist, depicting the past as distinct from the present but still a necessary component to understanding the present; (3) not teleological, meaning that the goal of history cannot and need not be known because we do not want to impose an agenda on the past so that we can champion an agenda for the future; and (4) broad in scope, although Ranke was largely concerned with the development of individual nations and their diplomatic interaction with other nations.

Ranke's emphasis on nations as the primary actors in history, and thus the central topic for investigation, was obviously a part of the contemporary preoccupation with national consolidations such as Germany and Italy. Ranke was broadly European in scope, but his followers narrowed the focus to individual nation-states. Trained as a philologist, Ranke defined acceptable source material very narrowly and thus limited the potential scope of history. Twentieth-century historians have expanded the scope of history by including topics such as climate or jealousy that previously would not have fallen under the historical rubric. Ranke then can be seen as the beginning of the modern historians in spite of the fact that the scope of his works was largely limited to the nation and the state.

NOTES

1. Frederick J. Turner, *The Significance of the Frontier in American History* (Ann Arbor, MI: University Microfilms, 1966; reprint of the edition first printed in the *Annual Report of the American Historical Association for the Year 1893*).

2. Anne Fadiman, *The Spirit Catches You and You Fall Down: A Hmong Child, Her American Doctors, and the Collision of Two Cultures* (New York: Farrar, Straus and Giroux, 1997).

3. Immanuel Wallerstein, *The Modern World-System: Capitalist Agriculture and the Origins of the European World-Economy in the Sixteenth Century* (New York: Academic Press, 1974).

4. Edward Shorter, "Capitalism, Culture, and Sexuality: Some Competing Models," *Social Science Quarterly* 53 (1972): 338–356. See also Shorter's "Sexual Change and Illegitimacy: The European Experience," in Robert J. Bezucha (ed.), *Modern European Social History* (Lexington, MA: D.C. Heath and Company, 1972), pp. 231–269.

5. Giambattista Vico, *The New Science*. Translation of the third edition (1744) by Thomas Goddard Bergin and Max Harold Fisch (Ithaca, NY: Cornell University Press, 1968); Johann Gottfried Herder, *Ideen zur Philosophie der Geschichte der Menschheit* (Darmstadt: Melzer, 1966). See also Immanuel Kant's 1774 review article "Idea for a Universal History from a Cosmopolitan Point of View."

Chapter 2

What Is History?

Suddenly the bulletin board on your roommate's side of the room catches your attention. The board is plastered with photos of your roommate's experiences at school. This collage of haphazard photos seems to lack any chronological organization. Photos were simply placed over edges of other photos. The range of photos reminds you of all the activities that have been important in your roommate's life since arriving at college. Your eyes stop on the occasional postcard, evidence that your roommate had ties to someone beyond the college. But the collage reveals nothing of your roommate's life before college. Below the bulletin board you notice a "photo album" style scrapbook. The first picture is the traditional high school graduation picture, a photo of one of life's milestones. But the remainder of the book catches you off guard. The second and third photos are tattered, old black and white photos of two different couples. The four people bear some resemblances to your roommate but not many. Next come photos of your roommate's parents. The clothes and hairstyles suggest that this was before your roommate even existed. Suddenly a pregnant mother and those frightening baby pictures. Did your roommate really wear those clothes and have that length of hair? More importantly, which set of pictures will offer more insight into your roommate's current whereabouts?

Both the collage and the photo album offer historical accounts of your roommate. A history written from the collage would likely be synchronic in that it encompasses a wide variety of your roommate's experiences. The photo album on the other hand is structured in a diachronic fashion moving from the grandparents straight through to your roommate's arrival at college. Which account offers a better perspective of the disappearance: pre-college development or college issues? Historians need to reconcile the obvious split between diachronic histories, which trace something over time, and synchronic histories, which place something into a wide context of diverse experiences and influences. Ranke's historicism focused on political development of European nations because that was a major issue facing thinkers in an age when Italy and Germany were becoming nations. Jacob Burckhardt, just one generation later, rejected Ranke's diachronic unfolding of history. Burckhardt's synchronic analysis of the Italian Renaissance offered a collage of the Italian Renaissance complete with sections on education, scientific discovery, society, festivals, morality, and religion. Burckhardt described politics as artistic expression[1] instead of as a diachronic unfolding of development. The scientific precision of diachronic historicism was challenged by the artistic evaluation of synchronic history because Burckhardt believed that viewing his subject from "the most varied points of view" would make the past more "intelligible."

The photo album contains an accurate unfolding of your roommate's life, yet the collage captures the emotion of your roommate's most recent experiences. Both sets of photos offer fragments of the same historical past. Historical artifacts, call them reality if you wish, are only interesting if one can project meaning into them. Just as the collage and photo albums are selective memories of your roommate's history, so too the insertion of meaning into the photo album and the collage involves emphasizing certain photos over others. History is essentially a selective memory. But then, what should be selected and what should be excluded? The director of a movie selects certain scenes and deletes others. This editing of film is done at the artistic discretion of the director. To what extent should historians employ artistic editing of the past? All photos of the past cannot be included; hence, some editing is required. How objective/subjective should one be? Is history an art or a science? What exactly are the limits of artistic freedom and the boundaries of scientific history? Or perhaps history is neither science nor art. Perhaps history is an autonomous form of knowledge that stands somewhere between the artistic and scientific extremes.

2.1 HISTORICAL FOCAL POINTS (DIACHRONIC VERSUS SYNCHRONIC HISTORY)

Ranke's hermeneutic history was achieved through empirical research of primary source material. His critical methods encouraged a positivistic tendency that led some followers to pursue a systematic methodology rivaling the scientific method. Simultaneous with this positivist tendency, Jacob Burckhardt, along with a handful of others of the generation after Ranke, consciously spurned the scientific model in favor of a more artistic approach that remained true to Ranke's hermeneutic historicism. Burckhardt cherished the "unscientific" nature of history, and his 1860 *The Civilization of the Renaissance in Italy* emphasized artistic over scientific explanations. In Part 1 of the book, "The State as a Work of Art," Burckhardt employed an art metaphor to lay a political foundation for his subsequent discussion of Renaissance individualism: "As the majority of the Italian states were in their internal constitution works of art, that is, the fruit of reflection and careful adaptation, so was their relation to one another and to foreign countries also a work of art."[2]

Burckhardt applied hermeneutic analysis and emphasized the uniqueness of the Renaissance, but his broader notion of acceptable sources allowed an examination of topics beyond the Rankean scope. Moreover, his use of a thematic approach involved synchronic analysis that differed from the diachronic unfolding of causal change that typified most historical accounts from his generation. This difference between the synchronic and diachronic approach is noteworthy because it constitutes a radically different method of conceptualizing the past: picture a timeline and then think of the diachronic as tracing one issue horizontally along that timeline, whereas the synchronic focuses on one point of that timeline but examines a much broader spectrum of issues.

The diachronic perspective is like viewing the past as a family photo album containing pictures of family members from different generations at various stages of development. Diachronic analysis focuses on how one factor, such as the family in the album, evolves from generation to generation. This focus allows the historian to chart growth and define specific change, but it fails to reveal the role of other factors. The synchronic analysis of process offers a montage of factors relevant to one specific generation of the family instead of tracing the family's evolution.

Burckhardt's analysis of a vertical cross section of society provides fewer details about the genealogical development of Renaissance politics, thought, science, religion, and society than would a diachronic approach to those specific topics, but the montage he creates by combining the topics expands the scope of history. Burckhardt's broadening of the scope of history and his insistence on the artistic side of the past have influenced generations of historians who have employed varying degrees of synchronic analysis. The extent to which a historian prefers synchronic or diachronic history is frequently related to the degree to which that historian views history as an artistic or a scientific pursuit.

2.2 HISTORY AS A FORM OF KNOWLEDGE (ART OR SCIENCE?)

The art-versus-science dichotomy was controversial long before Ranke and Burckhardt. Aristotle argued that history is inferior because it focuses on the particular instead of the general and universal.

Enlightenment thinkers, as discussed earlier, wanted to make history more scientific. Condorcet had scientific ambitions for history when he argued that human activities fall under regularities like other natural events and should therefore be studied scientifically. In the 1830s, Condorcet's optimistic assessment of scientific history and the future of humanity was modified by August Comte into a systematic progression through three stages: (1) the theological, (2) the metaphysical, and (3) the positive or scientific. Comte's three-stage teleological view was based on the belief that the positivistic pursuit of history, the third stage, would consist of observations leading to general laws governing human activity. Observations would reveal regularities that could be generalized into laws.

Comte's scientific progression influenced contemporaries of Burckhardt who emphasized the scientific over the artistic tendencies of history. Henry Thomas Buckle used Comte's theological, metaphysical, and scientific stages in volumes 1 and 2 of his unfinished *History of Civilization in England*. Buckle compared history to the other "branches of knowledge" and concluded that "history is still miserably deficient" because "the laws are unknown."[3] His debt to Comte is evident in the "General Introduction" where he poses three potential explanations for historical action: "Are the actions of men, and therefore of societies, governed by fixed laws, or are they the result either of chance or of supernatural interference?"[4] Comte's first two stages of development, the theological and metaphysical, appear in Buckle's descriptions of the supernatural interference and chance: (1) the "theological hypothesis" was a foundation for a "theory of Predestination" with its "doctrine of necessary connexion" or "supernatural interference," and (2) the "metaphysical hypothesis" was a foundation for a "theory of Free Will" with its "doctrine of Chance."[5] Buckle therefore developed the first two of Comte's stages into hypotheses upon which theories were founded and doctrines were proclaimed. The third alternative led to a scientific truth instead of doctrine, but you could collapse his discussion of inductive science, specifically statistics, to a hypothesis upon which the theory of uniformity and regularity would lead to fixed general laws:

Hypothesis	Theory	Doctrine
Theological →	Predestination →	Supernatural interference
Metaphysical →	Free will →	Chance
Scientific →	Uniformity →	Fixed laws

Buckle claimed that because we must reject

> the metaphysical dogma of free will, and the theological dogma of predestined events, we are driven to the conclusion that the actions of men, being

determined solely by their antecedents, must have a character of uniformity, that is to say, must, under precisely the same circumstances, always issue in precisely the same results.[6]

Thus, "the key and the basis of history" is the emulation of natural science with its pursuit of "universal order."[7] Human action is a product of the internal (man modifying nature) and the external (nature modifying man): "for since history deals with the actions of men, and since their actions are merely the product of internal and external phenomena, it becomes necessary to examine the relative importance of those phenomena."[8] Buckle's work turns to an examination of natural factors that influence humanity, such as climate, food, and soil.

This positivistic aspiration of progress, with its hope for improving the future, contrasted sharply with Rankean historicism, and thus the nineteenth century ended with historians more divided over the art-versus-science issue than at virtually any other time in history. John Bagnall Bury used his inaugural address as regius professor at Cambridge to discuss "The Science of History." He supported critical methodology and the positivist quest for generalization while admonishing the English tradition of history as literary expression of pedagogic morality. His conclusion that history was "simply a science, no less and no more" pushed George Macaulay Trevelyan to publish a short polemical defense of history as the "art of narrative" that should pursue "educative" purposes.[9]

Trevelyan dismissed the "history as science position" early and then moved to a description of history as pedagogic literary pursuit:

> I conclude, therefore, that the analogy of physical science has misled many historians during the last thirty years right away from the truth about their profession. There is no utilitarian value in knowledge of the past, and there is no way of scientifically deducing causal laws about the action of human beings in the mass. In short, the value of history is not scientific. Its true value is educational. It can educate the minds of men by causing them to reflect on the past.[10]

Trevelyan was more interested in human achievement than in accurate characterization of cause and effect:

> It is not man's evolution but his attainment that is the great lesson of the past and the highest theme of history. The deeds themselves are more interesting than their causes and effects, and are fortunately ascertainable with much greater precision. . . . And the story of great events is itself of the highest value when it is properly treated by the intellect and the imagination of the historian.[11]

This statement does not mean that the historian should not discuss cause-and-effect relationships, but rather that the narrative is more important: "It is the business of the historian to generalize and to guess as to cause and effect, but he should do it modestly and not call it *science*, and he should not regard it as his first duty, which is to tell the story."[12] The reason for telling stories is to educate a broad audience: "if historians neglect to educate the public, if they fail to interest it intelligently in the past, then all their historical learning is valueless except in so far as it educates themselves."[13]

He emphasizes nationalistic sentiment throughout both by critiquing other nations and championing the English:

> It is because the historians of today were trained by the Germanizing hierarchy to regard history not as an *evangel* or even as a *story*, but as a *science*, that they have so much neglected what is after all the principal craft of the historian—the art of narrative.[14]

Trevelyan believed that historical accounts should not be written for an audience of trained scientists or academics. History should be written for a general audience of average citizens.

Trevelyan went on to delineate five reasons for writing history to "educate the mind" of this national audience of the general public: (1) to put into perspective and "enlarge" the mind, (2) to remove prejudice and breed enthusiasm, (3) to present ideals and heroes, (4) to provide a background for understanding literature, and (5) to provide a background for travel (especially helpful for "the skilled game of identifying positions on a battlefield innocent of guides").[15] The educational side of history is more significant than extremist attempts to approach universal generalizations or purely artistic writings. History "has an element of both" art and science but with a restricted definition of each. It is neither science nor art, but a combination of three functions: (1) scientific—the gathering and sifting of facts, (2) imaginative or speculative—guesses and generalizations, and (3) literary—powerful narrative.

Trevelyan concluded the essay with the idea that "there is no 'verdict of history' other than the private opinion of the individual."[16] The relativistic tone evident throughout the essay is due in part to assumptions about the scope of history that were shattered by later historians. We will see how "microhistory" and "history from the bottom" are conscious rejections of his belief that

> in dealing even with an affair of which the facts are so comparatively well known as those of the French Revolution, it is impossible accurately to examine the psychology of twenty-five million different persons, of whom—except a few hundreds or thousands—the lives and motives are buried in the black night of the utterly forgotten. No one, therefore, can ever give a complete or wholly true account of the causes of the French Revolution.[17]

The title of Pierre Goubert's 1966 book *Louis XIV and Twenty Million Frenchmen* reveals the extent to which the scope of history has expanded.[18] Trevelyan therefore is not to be seen as a proponent of late twentieth-century relativism but as an example of the scope of "history" in the early twentieth-century debate about history versus science.

2.3 HISTORICAL CAUSATION

The turn-of-the-century science-versus-art dilemma failed to remain a controversial issue for most historians despite the fact that it was never successfully resolved. The debate was revived briefly in the 1940s when Carl Hempel, a philosopher of science, posited a "covering-law" theory of history in an essay entitled "The Function of General Laws in History."[19] Hempel argued that causation in history is understood by the use of deductive reasoning based on universal laws. The covering-law theory explains the writing of history with the same reasoning used in a syllogism such as "All humans are mortal, and Socrates is a human; therefore, Socrates is mortal." The covering law posits a general law followed by a particular and the ensuing result:

Law	If all a equals b	All humans are mortal
Particular	And c equals a	Socrates is a human
Result	Then c equals b	Socrates is mortal

Simply put, Hempel shows that when historians ask the question "why," they invoke a covering law by seeking causal arguments. Historical explanation is accomplished by constructing links between an event and its causes. These cause-and-effect links are based on regularities and patterns of behavior. If we only understand causation in terms of generalizations, such as the covering law, then historians do not examine individual events and people in and of themselves. History cannot therefore be concerned with the unique or particular in the absence of generalizations. Hempel and other covering-law theorists use the logic of the syllogism to argue that history should try to be scientific and to pursue the generalizations.

One problem with applying Hempel's covering law to history is that it does not depict what historians actually do. For instance, Crane Brinton approaches a Hempelian history in his *The Anatomy of Revolution* when he examines four revolutions (England in the 1640s, the United States in the 1770s, France in the 1780–1790s, and Russia in the 1910s).[20] He begins with generalizations about revolutions and concludes with "tentative uniformities" that are little more than meaningless generalizations such as that the government machinery was not functioning correctly (or it would have stopped the revolution) and many people lost faith in the government. Proponents of Hempel's method might argue that Brinton's shortcomings stem from a failure to apply Hempel's method as strictly as possible, but rigid applications, such as William Chandler's *The Science of History: A Scientific/Cybernetic Approach*, reveal other shortcomings. Chandler employed definitions, axioms, and hypotheses to analyze cybernetic history (communication and control processes). But he offered little more than "common sense" and tautological claims (a statement composed of simple points in a fashion that makes it true whether the simpler statements are true or false, such as "Either it will rain tomorrow or it will not rain tomorrow").[21] Strict application of covering laws to history has thus far not been able to overcome these tendencies toward meaningless generalizations, commonsense statements, and tautologies.

But the greatest problem facing covering-law theorists is that accepting covering-law theories about the past suggests that one should be able to predict the future, based on the past, because predictions follow the same structure as syllogisms; namely, the conditions are known, and one must simply look to the future. Hempel did modify his arguments later, but the early example we have cited fits clearly into the Enlightenment tradition of making history a science. On the other hand, the early position forced historians to sharpen their work by considering the role that theoretical assumptions played in the posing of basic historical questions. Historians are creatures of mass documents that they hope will lead to some conclusion, and Hempel forces them to think about how and why they structure logical arguments.

In the 1960s, a full twenty years after Hempel first posited his covering-law theory of history, quantitative history became a dominant field within history. Technological advances in early computing allowed historians to analyze quantitative data in new and exciting ways. Quantitative historians confidently predicted that the scientific analysis of quantitative data was the future of history. The growing popularity of quantitative history also sparked opponents of history-as-science, such as Hayden White, to champion the artistic, or literary, side of history. The pendulum swung back into the artistic side as "understanding" became more important than scientific cause-and-effect arguments.

2.4 THE STUDY OF HISTORY AS AN AUTONOMOUS DISCIPLINE

Historians seeking alternatives to the history-as-science position frequently champion the notion that history is an autonomous form of knowledge that is not any sort of science. In the late nineteenth century,

Wilhelm Dilthey argued that history does not equal science because scientists make something clear to an outside observer whereas historians attempt to understand things that are comprehensible from the perspective of the thing or action. Dilthey thus distinguished between the outsider's explanation (scientific *erklären*) and the insider's understanding (historical *verstehen*). Robin G. Collingwood offered an example of this autonomist position of historical knowledge in his book *The Idea of History*, published in 1946 three years after his death.[22] As an autonomous form of knowledge, history is the history of human thought. Historians should therefore consider history's impact on humans instead of the actual events themselves. In other words, historians should recreate the thoughts of people in history. This nonscientific approach asks for the sympathetic recovery of past actors' intuitions. The historian tries to understand an action from the perspective of the participants (what Brutus thought as he stabbed Caesar) instead of observing merely an object or event (the act of stabbing Caesar). This autonomist pursuit of historical knowledge obviously narrows the scope of history, but it is problematic for several other reasons:

1. History is limited to the history of articulate people in a manner that does not describe how contemporary historians actually practice (such as histories of climate or nature).
2. Collingwood's notions of understanding and sympathy pose moral dilemmas when one turns to a sympathetic understanding of deviants such as mass murderers (Collingwood gets this from the French proverb "If you understand it, you forgive it [or sympathize with it]"—*Tout comprendre, c'est tout pardonner*).
3. Evidence of past thought processes is also external to the mind of historical actors (we do not know a person's inner thoughts), so we can only have assumptions based on remnants such as inscriptions on tombstones.

The science-versus-art dilemma is broader than these two opposite approaches, but the differences, evident for instance in the positions of Hempel and Collingwood, offer provocative perspectives for historians to contemplate. On the eve of the twenty-first century, Thomas L. Haskell and others have revised these issues without contrasting narration with causation. Haskell emphasizes the similarities between the explanation model's "cause-and-effect" and the narration model's "beginning-middle-end." He contends that "narration is an especially supple form of causal reasoning."[23] Haskell thus separates causation from the universalizing covering laws.

Perhaps the best solution is simply to describe the dichotomy between art and science as false because it is built on erroneous assumptions about science and art. Thomas Kuhn and Robert Merton show that science does not exist as a timeless methodology: some sciences are as historical as history but are nonetheless scientific because of the historical aspect (such as evolutionary biology). If science is not actually practiced in the manner described by Hempel, then why should history be practiced scientifically?

NOTES

1. Jacob Burckhardt, *The Civilization of the Renaissance in Italy*, trans. S.G.C. Middlemore (London: Penguin Books, 1990). Part 1 is entitled "The State as a Work of Art."

2. Ibid., p. 73.

3. Henry Thomas Buckle, *History of Civilization in England*, vol. 1 (New York: D. Appleton and Company, 1858), p. 4.

4. Ibid., p. 6.

5. Ibid., pp. 6–10.

6. Ibid., pp. 14–15.

7. Ibid., p. 24.

8. Ibid., p. 26.

9. Trevelyan deleted all references to Bury when he republished the essay, after Bury's death, in his 1913 collection entitled *Clio, a Muse, and Other Essays* (London: Longmans, 1913), pp. 140–176.

10. Ibid., p. 147.

11. Ibid., p. 147.

12. Ibid., p. 148.

13. Ibid., p. 152.

14. Ibid., p. 148.

15. Ibid., pp. 152–158.

16. Ibid., p. 172.

17. Ibid., p. 144.

18. Pierre Goubert, *Louis XIV et vingt millions de Français* (Paris: Fayard, 1966).

19. For an early statement of Hempel's "rational scientific anticipation which rests on the assumption of general laws," see "The Function of General Laws in History," in *Theories of History*, ed. P. Gardiner (New York: Free Press, 1989), p. 349.

20. Crane Brinton, *The Anatomy of Revolution* (New York: W.W. Norton, 1938).

21. William Chandler, *The Science of History: A Scientific/Cybernetic Approach* (London: Gordon and Breach, 1984).

22. Robin G. Collingwood, *The Idea of History* (Oxford: Oxford University Press, 1994).

23. Thomas L. Haskell, *Objectivity Is Not Neutrality* (Baltimore: Johns Hopkins University Press, 1998), p. 14.

Chapter 3

Problems of Historical Knowledge: Historicism, Presentism, and the Writing of History

So where is your roommate? The entire situation has you feeling nauseous, and you fear that it is hindering your studies. You try to concentrate, but your mind wanders constantly to your roommate. The apartment haunts you as little items remind you of conversations, every facet of which seems to ricochet around in your memory. What about people who experience more traumatic events such as wars, floods, or imprisonment? Can someone who has not experienced severe sorrow or pain adequately describe tragic events? How can historians really describe reactions to the dropping of the first atomic bomb or the brutality of the Holocaust?

You decide to get out of the apartment and meet an old friend for dinner. Your friend insists on a complete "history" of the disappearance, and so you offer an "objective" account of the historical facts. During the course of your meal, you proceed to discuss these facts and to restructure the history. Your goal of objectivity is left behind as the conversation forces you to acknowledge and even address your friend's perspective. In fact, you find that rather than dealing with the past on its own terms you are now explaining the disappearance of your roommate in your friend's terminology. This may not seem to be a bold revision of history because your friend and roommate are contemporaries, but what would happen if the conversation were held sixty, or six hundred, years later? Would the values and terminology still reflect the perspective of the vanished roommate? Should you strive to frame everything from the perspective of the roommate, or would it be more meaningful to reconstruct the past utilizing your friend's terminology in order to calm your nerves and get on with your life? Should historians reconstruct the past on its own terms, or is the real reason for such a reconstruction to deal with present issues?

The presentist and historicist extremes are part of three fundamental ways of approaching the past:

1. the past was like the present, and human nature has not changed
2. the past was radically different from the present, so historians need to study it on its own terms
3. the past does not change but our understanding of it changes, so in effect the present determines the past.

The first alternative trivializes the study of history. Why should scholars examine the limited records of the past when the study of the present has so much fruitful evidence? Going to the past may reveal the trappings of exoticism, but other areas of study such as anthropology and sociology would be superior to history because they can examine the many facets of living subjects. Sociology and anthropology will be discussed in Chapter 4, but suffice it to say here that most historians find the second or third alternative more attractive because they believe that we are products of our distinctive period.

The second, or historicist's, approach to the study of history champions history as the one subject that allows us to understand how all knowledge has been constructed over time. Historicists seek to overcome their own subjectivity and to understand the past objectively on its own terms. Whether this objectivity is possible is the dilemma between the historicists and the presentists. Presentists embrace the third option and argue that we cannot break out of our perspective and free ourselves from subjective concerns.

The presentist position is strengthened by the teleological nature of history. Teleology, the development of progress or decline over time, is an inherent aspect of historical writing because historians are recounting a past after they know the outcome of it. Teleological history is certainly one of the most obvious temptations that historians face, but what about other temptations inherent in the act of retelling the past? The very act of telling a history entails having a beginning, a middle, and an end to the story. Do historians objectively select the beginning and end of a historical account, or does their choice of framework influence the history? The rhetorical and literary aspects of writing in general pose additional challenges for history beyond the questions of historicism and the taint of the present.

3.1 EXPERIENCING AND REMEMBERING THE PAST

If the goal of historians is to recover the past, then one would assume that objectivity would be the ultimate guide for historians. Historians would step outside their contemporary subjective values and offer interpretations of the past that are themselves timeless. Paul Fussell argues in "Thank God for the Atom Bomb" that the bombing of Hiroshima and Nagasaki is best understood not from the perspective of later moralists but rather from the perspective of "experience," namely, the perspective of soldiers who were in combat.[1] Fussell's historicism assumes that "understanding the past requires pretending that you don't know the present."[2] He contends that "historical memory" all too often "unwittingly" attempts "to resolve ambiguity and generally clean up the premises."[3] This form of revived historicism, known as neohistoricism, is based on the assumption that each age can only be understood on its own terms and that the goal is to uncover this specificity.

If all knowledge is historically determined, then do overarching standards of meaning exist? The inherent goal of uncovering the specificity of the past, as evident in the Chapter 1 analysis of Vico and Herder, becomes paramount when all knowledge is seen as historically constructed. The nineteenth-century historicism of Leopold von Ranke was based on the presupposition, or assumption, that the past was radically different from the present and that we must go to the past on its own terms. Modern neohistoricists reverse Aristotle's hierarchy and assume that history is the premier intellectual discipline that subsumes every other discipline. In that case, everything can only be understood, ultimately, in a historical context. The goal becomes returning to the past as it was instead of as we now understand it.

This neohistoricist position is buttressed by recent arguments that even the physical sciences evolve and develop historically. Thomas S. Kuhn's 1970 *The Structure of Scientific Revolutions* reveals that science can only be understood through historical analysis.[4] He claims that normal science currently progresses without structural questioning within an intellectual tradition, or paradigm. Paradigms allow scientists to explain their science, but they also shape the thinking of scientists. The slow appearance of exceptions to the paradigm, or anomalies as Kuhn calls them, eventually cast doubts on the value of the paradigm. The ensuing crisis makes that particular paradigm untenable and forces the creation of a new paradigm. In a scientific revolution, an entirely new framework of knowledge replaces former frameworks. Science within Kuhn's schemata therefore progresses by sharp paradigm ruptures rather than by steady incremental evolutions in knowledge. These "revolutions" offer a radical twist on the Hempelian notions discussed earlier because science ceases to be knowledge of the world as such and is rendered knowledge as formulated in terms of the particular paradigm in effect at any given moment. Thus, a significant element of scientific knowledge is historically contingent because it is determined by the paradigm rather than "reality."

Kuhn depicts scientists as pursuers of a reality within a given theory rather than as explorers of "truth." Scientists study reality within a paradigm's framework rather than "reality" in some Platonic sense. In essence, Kuhn argues for a historicity of science that supersedes the art-versus-science dichotomy that was analyzed previously. The art-versus-science dichotomy assumed that the two sorts of endeavors are fundamentally different: art is subjective, personal, and historically contingent, whereas science is impersonal, objective, and independent from history. Kuhn's scientific revolutions reveal the extent to which science is also historically contingent.

A more radical assault on traditional scientific knowledge is evident in Paul Feyerabend's rejection of a hierarchy of paradigms. The absence of hierarchy prevents us from distinguishing better paradigms. Feyerabend's reluctance to discuss the superiority of one paradigm constitutes a rejection of Hempel because we can only understand the way we go from one era to another without in any way delineating any concept of progress.

Feyerabend and others have therefore taken this to an extreme wherein different scientific paradigms and different kinds of knowledge (science versus magic, for instance) are equally valid. Consider the contrast between Hempel's insistence, in the art-versus-science debate, that history is a science and Kuhn and Feyerabend's insistence that in fact science can be understood only historically. The latter position has great value because it shows us how contingent knowledge is, and how we can understand it only in its context.

Vivid examples of the importance of context are evident in the way time and situation influence simple emotions that we take for granted and assume to be universal. A traditional, or hydraulic, view of emotions suggests that emotions are like liquids pent up within humans. At certain points the emotions swell and suddenly flow from us. The hydraulic view is remarkably similar to the traditional *humors* that preoccupied medieval thinkers. But, anthropological studies suggest that emotions may be something other than instinctive and natural. For instance, the Japanese believe in *amae*, an emotion associated with adults who take on an extreme "childlike" dependence. This emotion is normal and acceptable in Japan, but no similar regressive behavior exists in the Western European hierarchy of values. And within the Western tradition, emotions are contingent on both time and situation. The medieval emotion of *acedia* consisted of a simple sense of boredom with respect to one's religious obligations created by the dereliction of religious duties. *Acedia* was used to describe sloth and laziness in religious practice until the Protestant Reformation suddenly ended substantive descriptions of this emotion. Simply put, religious sloth and laziness became evidence of heresy rather than emotional constitution. Emotions may be instinctual reactions, but the expressions and descriptions of these instincts vary over time and place.

In the 1960s and 1970s, two competing views challenged the hydraulic theory of emotions; namely, a cognitive view and a social constructivist view.[5] The cognitive view believes that the capacity to have emotions is universal, but the expression of individual emotions is based on cultural norms and individual tendencies. Social constructivists contend that the display of emotions is formed and shaped by society. Some constructivists go so far as to reject the existence of internal mechanisms that produce emotions. The cognitive and constructivist views do not focus on restraint, the key component of the hydraulic view. Instead they focus on possibilities that cultures provide for the expression and representation of feelings. Loneliness offers a vivid example of how "natural emotions" may in fact be socially and historically constructed. The average college student is quite content to be alone on a Tuesday evening but is remarkably sad when alone on a Friday evening. Contentment and loneliness, then, appear to be either socially constructed or part of a process of perception and appraisal. The notion of hydraulic emotions that are permanent, natural, and given is rarely accepted by contemporary historians. Instead, emotions are viewed as (1) differing from culture to culture, (2) deriving from social values, and (3) changing over time. Emotions are in part culturally, socially, and historically contingent.

The implications of this historical and cultural contingency force historians to reconsider even the simplest given such as childhood. Has childhood always been an obvious and separate stage of human development? Philippe Ariès argued in *Centuries of Childhood* that children were not separate from adults during the Renaissance period, that they were treated as little adults. Pierre Riché places this evolution earlier than Ariès and claims that Renaissance children were already treated as separate from adults.[6] The psychohistorian Lloyd de Mause traced evolving conceptualizations of childhood and the treatment of children along a teleological timeline progressing from the ancient Greek practice of infanticide, to the Christian rejection of infanticide in the Middle Ages, to authoritarian child rearing in the nineteenth century, and last to the twentieth-century notion of "helping" relations between parents and children.[7] The significance of these studies from the historicist position is that they reveal the degree to which theories of childhood are historically contingent.

If theories of childhood are historically contingent, then would it not follow that notions of the family also varied enormously throughout history? The historicist pursuit of a past that is truly different from the present and understandable only on its own terms has produced a wealth of fruitful research as well as new sets of problems. The search for the otherness of the past frequently results in an emphasis on difference and an understatement of similarities. Furthermore, the delineation of otherness from historical records is problematic because all categories and standards have potentially changed. How does one discern the emotions of past generations? If parents observed their children fighting over toys in a day-care center, would they know whether the children were experiencing jealousy or envy? Psychologists have developed a simple experiment involving three people—A, B, and C. Person A is asked to observe and describe persons B and C sitting together at a café. Two specific cases are offered with radically different results. When B and C are defined as a romantic couple, then A experiences envy at the sight of the romantic couple B and C. When B and A are defined as a romantic couple, then A experiences jealousy at the sight of the beloved B sitting with C at the café. The distinction between envy and jealousy appears to be a product of the moral code of the society. This conclusion suggests that parents may not be able to distinguish accurately between jealousy and envy among small children because they are not full participants in the children's moral code.

Historicists assume the otherness of the past in order to avoid imputing modern values into the historical account. But how exactly does one delineate the values and emotions of historical actors who have left only fragmentary evidence of their existence? Furthermore, the historicists' assumptions of otherness encourage them to search for and emphasize differences, occasionally even at the expense of understating similarities. Does each new explanation of the past not create a new understanding of the past and therefore create a new historical past?

3.2 THE INDETERMINACY OF THE PAST

Every historicist study that clarifies a new otherness of the past creates a new understanding of the past and therefore creates a "new" historical past. Past actions are certainly fixed, but the interpretations of those actions change over time and thereby render historical accounts somewhat transmutable. Many historians do not want merely to recover the past, they seek to render a meaningful history of the past. Presentists argue that when historians write about the past they are actually writing for present concerns because they are unable to break out of themselves and their contemporary situation. The most radical conceptualizations of presentism are obviously controversial, but most historians would agree that the inherent teleological nature of history creates a presentist bias. At any given moment, historians are writing from an end point. Issues that are important to contemporaries need not be important later (and the converse is also true). New perspectives from the present change the past as everything in the past continually recedes into a larger pool.

The present influences the past because each new study changes our "knowledge" of the past. Presentism in this radical conceptualization is obviously controversial, but most historians would agree that the inherent teleological nature of history creates a presentist bias.

Describing the past with the terminology and values of the present obviously taints the past with presentist issues. Some extremists use presentist interpretations of the past in order to champion modern political agendas. Other presentists tend to focus on recent or modern events. The most obvious dangers of all presentism are the moral complacency and notions of superiority that arise from the insistence on championing present issues. On the other hand, historical accounts that fail to address present concerns are of relatively little value to society.

The inherent teleological nature of history forces historians to rewrite history from their own perspective, be it the history of (1) an era, such as the Enlightenment; (2) an event, like the French Revolution; or (3) a historical concept, such as genocide. Historical interpretations of the "Age of the Enlightenment" and "Enlightenment optimism" have fluctuated greatly over time. Early positive assessments of the Enlightenment emphasized the pursuit of rationality, the beginning of belief in progress, and the optimistic notion that the world could be understood and accordingly changed. Historians of the Enlightenment frequently overlook the popular rise of Pietism and Methodism, religious beliefs that are not consistent with these Enlightenment ideals. Enlightenment assessment in the twenty-first century varies greatly and is in part a product of personal ideology, but few historians describe the Enlightenment with the optimistic assessment that was prevalent one hundred years ago. Certainly the implementation of Enlightenment ideas contributed to a series of twentieth-century disasters such as two "world wars" and the Holocaust. Contemporary historians have a different perspective on the "Age of the Enlightenment" than did historians in 1900 simply because they are living at a later time.

Modern events cause historians to look at past events and concepts differently as well. Historical accounts of the French Revolution were altered drastically after the Russian Revolution provided a new context for interpreting revolutions. The French Revolution ceased to be considered a middle-class victory that cleared the economic floor and spurred the era of middle-class industrial democracy. Just as the Russian Revolution created a new context for interpreting the events of the French Revolution, so too the Jewish Holocaust created a new context for historical terminology such as "genocide." The historical concept of genocide was initially coined by French historians to describe the drowning of masses of counterrevolutionaries in the French Revolution. Early forms of genocide were conceived as examples of revolutionary politics run amok. The late twentieth-century usage is markedly different because of the rise of Hitler and his implementation of the Jewish Holocaust. The present always changes, and in so doing, it may change the way historians understand and describe the past.

Modern events do not change the past, because technically the past cannot change, but they create new perspectives and thereby change our understanding of the past. All historical accounts contain a presentist aspect because teleology is inherent in history. The past is concrete, but how we record and explain it is not; hence, the present determines the shape of the past.

We cannot break out of ourselves, our environment, or our teleological perspective, but to what extent should historians attempt to be presentist? Hans-Georg Gadamer argues in *Truth and Method* that we cannot reach objectivity because all knowledge is relative.[8] Can we only know ourselves? The prejudices of the present function much like a race horse's "blinders" that prevent us from discussing history objectively. Gadamer stresses "the way the being of the interpreter pertains intrinsically to the being of what is interpreted."[9] History then is irremediably locked into presentist concerns, and historians cannot realistically hope to free themselves from their own subjectivity.

Attempting to recreate the past on its own terms becomes futile because you cannot reconstruct those historical terms. Consider, for instance, an attempt to rebuild a house that was destroyed by a flood. One could purchase all of the "original" materials and construct a new house on the old spot, but, even if the original materials were available, it would be a new replica with the requisite problems of a new house. One simply cannot reconstruct the original house, but one can construct a replica that has clear similarities and differences.

An extreme formulation of Gadamer's position leads to radical subjectivism that borders on solipsism. Solipsism theorizes that the self is the only thing that can be verifiably known. Humans become the measure of all things, and solipsists refuse to believe anything outside of themselves. Everything external becomes a figment of the imagination. All knowledge is relative, and we can only know ourselves. The futility of this position derives from an understanding that history does exist and that extreme presentism does nothing to improve our understanding of the past. A radical formulation of Gadamer's position is thus fruitless.

The historicism–presentism debate can be formulated as a continuum with two poles: neohistoricists attempt to overcome all subjectivism whereas strong presentists claim that historians cannot possibly free themselves from their own subjectivity. The most fruitful solution to the historicist–presentist debate exists somewhere between these extremes. One logical solution would be to reconcile presentism and historicism by acknowledging that presentism is inherent while striving for historical perspective based on the past's own terms.

3.3 REWORKING THE PAST

The presentist–historicist debate is further complicated by the actual writing of history; namely, the literary aspect of writing history. Twentieth-century theories of language and literature challenged the distinctions between history and fiction. Some philosophers went so far as to argue that knowledge does not just reflect reality; it actually creates this reality in the process of knowing it. We will examine postmodernism in detail in Chapter 7, but for now it is worth considering the role of language in mediating knowledge and determining reality.

People who speak only one language often take for granted the way that their language functions. Students of two or more languages usually realize that languages use gender and past tenses in slightly different ways. The structure of a language influences how one speaks and writes about other people and about the past. A speaker of English is forced to insert gender into a conversation when she/he uses a pronoun. For instance, if someone wandered into your history class and asked "Is this French 201?" you might well describe what happened as "a person came into our class and she/he asked if this was a French class." The English language forces speakers to view the person as he or she and to identify the person accordingly. But in the French 201 classroom, the person would be labeled as feminine and given the pronoun *elle* regardless of the person's gender. The French word *personne* is feminine and the corresponding pronoun is the equivalent of the English "she." The structural differences between two languages of the same family (English and French are both Indo-European languages) result in different ways of explaining the presence of a person in the classroom with English forcing the speaker to seek the gender of the person.

Differences between languages will frequently be greater when one compares two languages from different families such as English and Finnish. English speakers use she/he as a pronoun for people but also for other things such as animals and vehicles. Finnish uses a different pronoun for a person (*hän*) than for a nonhuman (*se*), but neither pronoun includes any sense of gender. A person is *hän* regardless of her/his gender. Native speakers of Finnish who learn English later in life will frequently mix the pronouns she/he in a manner that is baffling to native speakers of English. Native speakers of English spend a lifetime making decisions about a person's gender each time they employ the pronouns she/he whereas speakers of Finnish only need to contemplate a person's gender when the issue of gender is part of the conversation. Languages thus have structures that influence the way that people talk about reality.

Stanford University psychologist Lera Boroditsky studies how language shapes thought. Her focus on mental representation, metaphoric structuring, and past tenses in different languages suggests that even our notions of causality may be influenced by language. This goes far beyond the generally accepted notion that something may be lost in translation. The implications for history move historians beyond Ranke's simple notion of "how it actually happened" when one realizes that differences over time and between languages will influence how we talk about the past both in our own language and in other languages. An historian of Finland who writes in English is forced to write a text that makes distinctions that would be foreign to a Finnish person from the past. The past is reworked both when it is put into a different language and when it is explained in the same language over time.

The plethora of languages, and even meanings for words within one language, suggest that words do not have meaning because they contain a relationship to some preexisting and objective reality. Rather, the meaning of a word is constituted by the whole system of language itself. Shakespeare employed a metaphor when he wrote "All the world's a stage." This figure of speech is based on an implicit comparison of two different things: a world and a stage. The metaphor allows the speaker to clarify reality by means of these comparisons. Metaphors are linguistic rhetorical devices that help constitute the way we actually see the world. Language then structures reality because an observer translates observations into concepts and then translates them further into words. Language determines reality because language determines the range of possible ways to conceptualize that reality.

Ferdinand de Saussure examined the structure of language. He distinguished between *langue* (language), or the linguistic system that all speakers utilize unconsciously, and *parole* (speech), the actual utterances that people produce. In all linguistic systems, language consists of the signified (the mental concept) and the signifier (the spoken word). The signified, or concept, is part of a preexisting conception of something whereas the signifier, or word, refers back not to the object itself but rather to the concept (the signified). Signifiers (words) only have meaning within the network of a language (the signs). The link between the signifier and signified is arbitrary, which allows for confusion in language. This confusion is more acute in written communication than in spoken communication because when people speak to each other they communicate with more than just words. Spoken communication includes nods, facial expressions, and body language, which contribute to understanding. Written communication lacks the extra information and thus is more susceptible to misunderstanding.

Each signified (mental concept) corresponds to a signifier (word), but a word can have more than one meaning (more than one signified). Spoken communication allows the speaker and listener to include nonverbal communication and thus is better than written communication.

Spoken communication allows for more accurate understanding of the concepts (the signified). This makes the meaning of words less confusing in spoken than in written communication because a written text does not include any such clues. De Saussure's structuralism privileged spoken communication over written communication. Later in the book we will consider how Roland Barthes reversed this relationship with his semiology or science of signs. Barthes severed the connection between the author's conception of reality and the text. Jacques Derrida, in the late twentieth century, took the "language determines reality" position even further. The meaning of any given word is determined not by its alleged referent in reality, but by its reference to other words, which in turn only refer to other words, and so on.

Derrida contends that no one meaning for any given text exists. In other words, there is no way to say which meaning is definitively true. Hence, the author, the individual behind the text, ceases to be important: the connection between the text and the author is severed as text disappears into an intertextuality that always refers back to other texts. What the author meant to say has no privileged position among the various ways a text can be interpreted. The act of interpretation of a text thus becomes more important than the writing of the text.

The distinction between history and fiction proves to be fiction itself. The implications for history are staggering: (1) the disappearance of the author and the historical actor as coherent subjects, (2) the disappearance of the text as something with a discernible meaning, and (3) the disappearance of any teleology in history.

Postmodernists make us aware that the literary aspect of history involves biases just as the radical subjectivism and skepticism of Gadamer revealed the naiveté of historians' ambitions of understanding a text or an event in its historical context. Postmodernists therefore show us that historical writing is subject not only to subjectivist biases but also to rhetorical and literary aspects of writing (such as the opening and closing of a book or chapter). But if postmodernism further relativizes the writing of history, does it also mean that all viewpoints are equally valid? How are we to refute viewpoints that we find reprehensible, morally or politically, in the ensuing free-for-all? Postmodernists offer no Archimedean point and therefore no real lever for creating change.

The absence of an Archimedean point generates problems when historians tackle moral issues, such as how to interpret the Holocaust. Chapter 2 of this book ended with a brief discussion of the autonomist pursuit of history and how Collingwood's notions of understanding and sympathy posed moral dilemmas when applied to a sympathetic understanding of Nazism (*tout comprendre, c'est tout pardonner*). The inherent sympathizing or forgiving of reprehensible actions is now further compounded by the postmodernist failure to offer any foundation for condemning reprehensible interpretations of those actions. Frequently this is not an issue because the contemporary audience may have no vested interest in the morality of many historical actors. But other topics are more controversial and require fervent and vigilant rejection of some interpretations. The 1980s German "historians' debate" over assessments of Germany's recent past, specifically the degree to which Nazism and the Holocaust were unique, is a prime example of how the creation of historical consensus forces historians to monitor themselves and maintain standards of acceptable history.

The German "historians' debate," or literally "quarrel among historians" (*Historikerstreit*), is about the reworking of history and the limits to that reworking. Initially it involved historians and philosophers examining the role that the Nazi period, and especially the Holocaust, should play in German history. President Ronald Reagan's 1985 visit to Bitburg, a German cemetery, on the fortieth anniversary of the German surrender, is an example of the broader political and popular sphere of interest. One consequence of Germany's exclusion from a June 1984 D-Day anniversary celebration was that German Chancellor Helmut Kohl asked President Reagan to acknowledge Germany's wartime losses with a visit to Bitburg and Dachau. The White House accepted a visit to Bitburg but rejected the Dachau visit, and then at a March 21 news conference President Reagan explained: "The German people have very few alive that remember even the war, and certainly none that were adults and participating in any way."[10] Reagan's own age proved that claim to be wrong, and the White House later agreed to visit the Bergen-Belsen concentration camp. The Bitburg cemetery visit was further complicated by the fact that it contained the graves of Waffen SS soldiers. The ensuing public discussion of such a visit was just one of a wide range of issues that challenged popular assessments of history's role in contemporary Germany.

Other notable controversies included German politician Philipp Jenninger's resignation in 1988, after protests about his speech at the fiftieth anniversary of the organized pogroms of *Kristallnacht*, and heated public exchanges over the content of museums and theaters such as the outcry over the Frankfurt staging of Reiner Werner Fassbinder's play *Der Müll*. One phase of the 1980s controversies was the specifically academic "historians' debate" that was provoked in part by a subtitle to one collection of key documents: "The Uniqueness of the National Socialist Annihilation of the Jews." This debate was not about specific facts or about general theories of morality; it centered on the origins and explanations of Nazi atrocities. It raised fundamental issues of historical causality, context, and comparability that directly confront our somewhat theoretical examination of presentism, historicism, the indeterminacy of the past, and the reworking of the past.

Reagan's Bitburg remarks in May 1985 reflected an interpretation of the Third Reich as "one man's totalitarian dictatorship." This antiquated and discarded historical thesis had served to cleanse the general population of significant guilt because it implicated Hitler as an evil ruler who was forced unwittingly upon the population. Reagan's failure to offer comparative examples further suggested that the Third Reich was unique and Hitler was a historical anomaly. This interpretation of the Third Reich is almost diametrically opposite to that championed by conservative German historians such as Ernst Nolte. Simultaneous with the Bitburg speech, a Nolte article entitled "Between Myth and Revisionism? The Third Reich in the Perspective of the 1980s" appeared in an English-language anthology.[11] Nolte argued that "revision" is inherent in historical writing and that it was time to review the known facts about the Third Reich, not to overturn them but to reconsider them in a larger historical context. Nolte suggested that Hitler's egregious treatment of Jews as enemies of war might be justified by the fact that Chaim Weizmann said in September 1939 that Jews would support the democracies in case of war. The absurdity of this one point allows critics to dismiss it easily without grappling with the broader issue posed by Nolte: What is the correct framework for understanding the Nazis?

Throughout his writings, Nolte has sought to put the Third Reich into a broader twentieth-century perspective. His 1976 book *Germany and the Cold War* argued that (1) Nazi mass murders are causally linked to the Bolshevik atrocities, which were known to Hitler in the 1920s; hence, Hitler's "racial murder" was preceded factually and logically by Bolshevik "class murder"; and (2) Hitler committed mass murder in part because he and the Nazis perceived themselves as potential targets of mass murder; hence, Hitler's actions are not legitimate, but it is wrong "to look at only one mass murder and not take into account the other, when a causal nexus between them is probable."[12] Nolte's attempts to relativize the Third Reich, within the framework of twentieth-century normality, and specifically his constructions of causal ties to the Bolsheviks were not new when a leading newspaper, the *Frankfurter Allgemeine Zeitung*, published his short article in June 1986 entitled "The Past That Will Not Pass Away." In it, Nolte undermines the distinctiveness of the Holocaust and claims that the contemporary preoccupation with the Holocaust served the interests of younger Germans against their fathers' generation as well as "the interests of the persecuted and their descendants in a permanent privileged status."

German philosopher Jürgen Habermas responded to Nolte's newspaper article in an attack against Nolte and other historians, most notably Andreas Hillgruber.[13] He dismissed Nolte's points and rejected Hillgruber's empathy for participants of the Third Reich. Hillgruber is best known for efforts to delineate the direction and timing of Hitler's expansionist plans. He was one of the first historians to attempt to connect Hitler's attack on the Soviet Union to the policy of killing Jews. His attempts to show the logic of Hitler and the Nazis blurred the distinction between understanding and justifying those actions. Hillgruber's ideas were also not new, but he had recently published a small book that juxtaposed the Nazi genocide against the Jews with analysis of the German army on the Soviet front (*Two Types of Decline: The Destruction of the German Reich and the End of European Jewry*).[14] Habermas rejected the tone and method of constructing a sympathetic understanding of Nazism. Furthermore, he claimed that the *Frankfurter Allgemeine Zeitung* published outlandish interpretations of the Third Reich because they were easily manipulated by the "ideology planners" who needed "images of the enemy" in order to forge a national consensus. He lumped Nolte and Hillgruber together with a group of German historians who he believed were revising the past in order to create a patriotic nationalism that coincided with a general conservative shift in German politics. The political shift, known as the *Wende* that had ushered in Helmut Kohl's Christian Democrats, slowly influenced the humanities as some museums and publicly funded art programs fell under the control of conservative political appointments.

Participants in the historians' debate could be divided into two general camps consistent with their political affiliations. Christian Democrats and center-right historians tended to support the comparative method and thus interpreted the Third Reich as part of a twentieth-century phenomenon that was broader than Nazi Germany. They believed that it was time to integrate Hitler's reign into a broader pattern of German development in order to prevent it from distorting national self-identity. The Social Democrats and liberal-left historians opposed such assimilation because they believed it was part of a nationalist failure to grapple with the atrocities of the Third Reich and the unique German situation that allowed Hitler to rise to power. They recognized that some form of comparison is inevitable in the writing of history but that comparisons with the Bolsheviks were faulty and apologetic.

The German historians' debate offered a rare opportunity for a public exchange, largely in newspapers in this instance, among historians struggling to keep other historians in check. The broader newspaper-reading audience that participated largely as observers in the debate took a more active role in a later episode. In August 1996, a German translation of Daniel Goldhagen's *Hitler's Willing Executioners* was published, and sales in Germany and Austria took off.[15] The ensuing book tour witnessed huge crowds gathered to hear the American's comments about his rather simple thesis: average Germans were willing executioners because German culture included a unique eliminationist anti-Semitism. Goldhagen shattered the traditional historical account of a mechanistic dehumanized killing of Jews by a small group of know-ing accomplices and replaces it with the idea that the perpetrators were a "representative cross section of German men" and thus were "repre-sentative of Germans" in general. He hinted at the potential historical controversy in the Epilogue:

> That the eliminationist antisemitic German political culture, the genesis of which must be and is explicable historically, was the prime mover of both the Nazi leadership and ordinary Germans in the persecution and extermination of the Jews, and therefore was the Holocaust's principal cause, may at once be hard to believe for many and commonsensical to others.[16]

The popular success of the book occurred despite the fact that German historians and the German press in general had been highly critical of the English-language release earlier that same year. German review-ers had attempted to dismiss the book by labeling it unoriginal, based on shoddy research, and the propagandistic criticism of the son of a Holocaust survivor. The book has its obvious shortcomings—reviewers from outside Germany were quick to delineate dubious causal relations and exaggerated conclusions—but the popular reaction to the German translation forced a reevaluation of the work by German historians and intellectuals.

This example of popular interpretations differing from professional historians' interpretations raises the broader issue of the general perti-nence of history. The context of a general 1980s shift toward conservative politics in Germany, as in the United States and Great Britain, reveals the extent to which questions of national self-identity are political. The political context suggests that to a certain degree the historians' debate is about academics participating in a cultural discussion about nationalism and even Germany's participation in NATO. Peter Baldwin's summa-tion of the historians' debate poses a broader significance:

> The most important theme that it raises concerns the inevitability of a new coming to terms with Germany's recent past, for Germans and for others alike. . . . There is no historical statute of limitations after which a "normal" perspective will set in once again. The question is not when will Nazism finally be viewed as part of history as usual, for that day is unlikely ever to come, but how will this period, with all its anguish and inexplicability, be situated within our collective memory.[17]

The fact that this topic has demanded so much consideration among professional historians and the general public led one senior American historian, Charles Maier, to conclude that "the point is that the grow-ing acceptance of postmodern criteria for what constitutes historical knowledge has legitimated the new revisionism. The fashions of historiography have altered, but quality goods and shoddy can still both find a market."[18] How historians esteem Maier's "fashions" remains an open question, although he prefers a postmodern historicization that poses "the aesthetic evocation of earlier repression in the name of historical understanding."[19] Baldwin optimistically points out that "the debate should be welcomed as evidence that Nazism and its horrors are far from having been swallowed up by forgetfulness."[20] In the coming chapters we will look at a quagmire of historical "fashions" so that you can make informed judgments about the potential styles of history.

NOTES

1.   Paul Fussell, "Thank God for the Atom Bomb," in *Thank God for the Atom Bomb and Other Essays* (New York: Summit Books, 1988), pp. 13–37.

2.   Ibid., p. 24.

3.   Ibid., p. 14.

4.   Thomas S. Kuhn, *The Structure of Scientific Revolutions*, 2nd edn. (Chicago: University of Chicago Press, 1970).

5.   For more on how historians have viewed human emotions see Barbara H. Rosenwein's article "Worrying about Emotions in History,"*The American Historical Review*, 107 (June 2002).

6.   Pierre Riché and Danièle Alexandre-Bidon, *L'enfance au Moyen Age* (Paris: Seuil, Bibliothèque nationale de France, 1994).

7.   Lloyd de Mause, *The History of Childhood* (Northvale, NJ: J. Aronson, 1995). Originally published in 1974 by Psychohistory Press.

8.   Hans-Georg Gadamer, *Truth and Method*, translation revised by Joel Weinsheimer and Donald G. Marshall, 2nd rev. edn. (London: Sheed and Ward, 1989).

9.   Hans-Georg Gadamer, *Reason in the Age of Science* (Cambridge, MA: MIT Press, 1981), p. 136.

10.   President's News Conference on Foreign and Domestic Issues, *New York Times*, March 22, 1985, p. A12.

11.   Hannsjoachim W. Koch, ed., *Aspects of the Third Reich* (New York: St. Martin's Press, 1985).

12.   Ernst Nolte, *Deutschland und der Kalte Krieg*, 2nd edn., (Stuttgart: Klett-Cotta, 1985).

13.   Jürgen Habermas's article appeared in the November 7, 1986, edition of the German weekly *Die Zeit*. The article was translated into English as "A Kind of Settlement of Damages (Apologetic Tendencies)", in *New German Critique* 44 (Spring/Summer 1988).

14.   Andreas Hillgruber, *Zweierlei Untergang: die Zerschlagung des Deutschen Reiches und das Ende des europäischen Judentums* (Berlin: W.J. Siedler, 1986).

15.   Daniel J. Goldhagen, *Hitler's Willing Executioners: Ordinary Germans and the Holocaust* (New York: Random House, 1996).

16.   Ibid., p. 454.

17.   Peter Baldwin, *Reworking the Past: Hitler, the Holocaust, and the Historian's Debate* (Boston: Beacon Press, 1990), p. 29.

18.   Charles S. Maier, *The Unmasterable Past: History, Holocaust, and German National Identity* (Cambridge, MA: Harvard University Press, 1988), p. 170.

19.   Ibid., p. 172.

20.   Baldwin, *Reworking the Past*, p. 30.

Chapter *4*

Cross-Pollination

Individuals usually take action without consideration of how social scientists or historians will interpret that action. For instance, consider the meal you ate at the beginning of the last chapter when you met a friend. Why that restaurant? Why did you order what you ordered? Once you have answered those questions, turn to considerations of how historians or social scientists might interpret your actions. Social scientists could focus on economic factors or on cultural factors that have no relationship to economic calculation.

The range of possible interpretations is quite astounding. One interpretation could be purely quantitative, whereas another might have nothing to do with mathematics. And even the quantitative interpretations may vary from statistical analysis of restaurant visits to economic analysis of your income or perceived class. Statistical perspectives might place your individual action into a broader, aggregate context of restaurant visits to reveal patterns in your behavior of which you may not be aware. Another quantitative perspective could be economic or materialist: you chose the restaurant because it was inexpensive. Even your choice of food was contingent on price as you passed over some excellent selections that were "too expensive" for you. Some social scientists might ignore quantitative factors and focus instead on normative or ideological considerations. You chose the restaurant because it served the kind of food to which you are accustomed. Your choice of food was contingent on internal norms of taste that developed in your family or society. Yet another interpretation would suggest that basic needs were the determining factor. You chose the restaurant because it was nearby, and your choice of food was contingent on your degree of hunger. This interpretation even allows for materialist and normative judgments within the broader assumption that your biological needs were the main determining factor. In fact, proponents of this functional theory may argue that those judgments were nothing more than a product of other needs.

Perhaps some mixture of statistical, materialist, normative, or functional reasoning is necessary to explain your decisions, but you must decide which factors were the most significant and why they were.

Does the very act of considering these four broad means of explanation influence the way that you might interpret a past action? Do they not force you to reconsider your previously stated explanation? Is your restaurant visit better understood in light of new theories, or have theories confused the issue by suggesting reasoning that seems more plausible than your initial explanation? After all, why should a theory cause you to alter your explanation of your own experience? The "facts" about your restaurant visit have not changed, but your interpretation of that action may have changed. This exercise should help you recognize that others could interpret your actions in a rational way that has nothing to do with your stated intentions or rationale.

Statistics, economics, sociology, and anthropology are certainly too complicated for mere reduction to these four means of explanation, but such a reduction does offer a simple starting point for evaluating these fields of study and their influences on history. The measures of actions and intentions in this case are reducible to four general methods:

1. the statistical method suggests that the aggregate analysis reveals patterns that may not be evident when studying a small pool of inhabitants;
2. the materialist, or economic, explanation suggests that economic calculation is the best measure;
3. the normative explanation suggests that societal values are the most significant; and
4. the theory of human or anthropological needs suggests that action and intention can be reduced to basic human drives.

Each explanation allows for a wide range of interpretations. There is no shortage of debate within each of these broad groupings. For instance, quantification can involve basic studies of population statistics, or it can follow the mathematical models of the New Economic Historians. Economics can be simple quantitative calculation, or it can follow some version of Karl Marx's notions of class and economic determinism. The sociological approach could involve Emile Durkheim's idealism or Max Weber's attempts to incorporate materialist and voluntarist explanations. The anthropological approach could involve functionalist-anthropologist Bronislaw Malinowski's emphasis on the biological determinants of cultural action. All of these explanatory schemata offer perspectives that are not evident in competing models.

The four paradigms, or schemata, listed earlier have been successfully employed by twentieth-century historians to explain historical change. The cross-pollination of history and disciplines noted for stricter methodologies forces contemporary historians to make complicated decisions about methodology. In employing one explanation, a historian is implicitly suggesting that the chosen explanation is better than the other three. The cross-pollination of history thus has forced historians to reconsider the methodological implications of their work. This focus on methodology has prevented historians from becoming too smug in their interpretations of the past.

4.1 CLIOMETRICS: QUANTIFICATION AND HISTORY

In Chapter 2, we looked at British historian George Macaulay Trevelyan's defense of Clio, the muse of history. Trevelyan's argument in favor of artistic history corresponded with a range of similar attacks on the presuppositions of scientific history from historians across the European continent. Italian philosopher and historian Benedetto Croce wrote an influential essay in 1893 championing history as art. Meanwhile, the scientific camp was fortified in France with Henri Berr's attempts to make history into the synthesizing branch of the emerging social sciences. Berr argued that history is scientific because historians explain what happened and why, instead of simply contenting themselves with descriptions. Historians do not collect facts; they connect them into explanations of the past. This connection of historical data to explanations involved synthesis based on a logic or method of understanding. Berr's vision of a history of science involved the fastidious collection of facts that would then be synthesized in a manner consistent with generalizations or laws. The resulting historical analysis would be scientific but not deterministic.

In the 1890s, Paul Lacombe argued in French and Karl Lamprecht argued in German that history passed from a prescientific phase to a scientific phase. In the prescientific phase, historians used individual methods and gathered individual facts whereas historians in the scientific phase synthesized those facts into generalized explanations. Some subfields within history, notably economic, social, and demographic history, lend themselves to a form of quantitative analysis whereby historians isolate and quantify significant variables that are capable of general explanations of change.

Cliometrics is the application of quantitative methods (metrics) to historical topics (Clio, the muse of history). The basic premise is that the statistical analysis of quantifiable variables will reveal patterns that would otherwise remain hidden. Patterns are revealed in the aggregate that are not visible in the individual. Immanuel Kant's *Idea for a Universal History from a Cosmopolitan Point of View* is an early example of the emphasis on aggregate history instead of individual history. Kant claimed that while individuals may believe that free will rules their destiny, individual action is part of broader patterns and laws governing society. Patterns within those societies reveal that many factors—such as births, marriages, and deaths—remain remarkably constant despite individuals' purported exercise of free will. Buckle's quantification of suicides (see Chapter 2), or even the number of letters that are sent without addresses on the envelope, provides evidence of patterns that are only visible in the aggregate.

The late nineteenth century and the 1950s–1960s were two important periods of intensive interest in quantitative history that offer a perspective on the extent to which the cross-fertilization of history with other fields, such as statistics, influences all historians. Cliometricians have claimed to solve all methodological problems, while nonquantitative historians have denied their claims to being historians at all. In the late nineteenth century, cliometricians claimed that it was no longer possible to practice history in the old way. Their methodological arrogance demanded a level of professionalization that challenged history as a "gentlemanly" profession requiring little more than a background in liberal arts.

The shift in history, noted by Lacombe and Lamprecht among others, from a prescientific phase of "fact gathering" to a scientific phase of synthesis and explanation was part of this general professionalization of history. Any well-read person would have been considered a historian simply by reading and writing history. The absence of mandatory specialized training, such as was required for the legal or medical profession, meant that historians were a fairly conservative lot because senior historians could easily dismiss the writings of younger historians who did not share their views. Cliometricians threatened to limit history to a full-time profession of trained specialists.

The ensuing professionalization of history corresponded with a democratization of the subject of history as historians turned from analysis of great individuals to the role of the masses. This democratization was also directly linked to the professionalization because the reliance on professional historians allowed more room for dissent than had previously existed. The conservative tradition that filtered out well-read younger historians for holding extreme views slowly evolved into a field full of professionals who could employ acceptable methods to further more radical views. But this shift also limited the prospective audience to readers with sufficient background in methodology.

The 1950s–1960s revival of quantitative methods enhanced the distance between the general history-reading public and professionals who had been trained in statistics. Many quantitative methods exist, but attaining statistically significant analysis requires fairly sophisticated mathematics. Data that had previously been utilized for one specific context were now manipulated into "sampling" techniques that spoke for a much broader context. One particular movement, the New Economic Historians, moved beyond quantification of economic records to the creation of economic models that could be tested. These historians constructed statistical models from periods with sufficient quantitative data and then used those models to analyze other times and places.

For instance, Fernand Braudel lacked statistics for the entire Mediterranean region, so he used the available information to construct a model. The data were not sufficient for an acceptable sample, based on mathematical sampling, but he could construct a model that could then be tested via computer simulation. He described the sixteenth-century Mediterranean economy as follows: *population*: 60 million; *urban population*: 6 million or 10%; *gross product*: 1,200 million ducats per year or 20 ducats per head; *cereal consumption*: 600 million ducats, half of the gross product; *government taxes*: 48 million ducats or below 5% of average income.[1] The use of a wide range of limited sources allowed him to construct a model or general outline of the economic situation.

Perhaps the most controversial use of mathematical models by historians following the New Economic History methodology was the construction of counterfactual hypotheses that could then be tested against the available source material. The use of statistics to support these models proved to be a powerful way to challenge and even dispel commonly held positions. For instance, Robert W. Fogel constructed a model of nineteenth-century America without railroads in order to show that economic development would have continued down a similar path even if alternative modes of transportation had been used instead of the railroads. He dispelled the accepted theory that the railroad was the crucial factor in America's economic development.

Fogel teamed with Stanley L. Engerman in a very controversial 1974 book entitled *Time on the Cross: The Economics of American Negro Slavery*.[2] The book is significant not only for its use of quantitative analysis to challenge an accepted historical truth but also because of the political overtones of its conclusions. Fogel and Engerman attacked the assumption that American slavery was an economically irrational institution— namely, that slavery was not profitable and therefore slaveholders must have had motives for defending slavery that were not economic. In other words, historians had assumed that the slave system was not economically sound and thus believed that slaveholders went to war to defend their way of life and maintain prestige and honor.

Fogel and Engerman utilized quantitative evidence in their argument to show that slavery was a profitable investment for slaveholders.

Their comparative analysis of investments in Northern industry with investments in Southern slaveholding suggested that slaveholding was profitable. If the system slaveholders were fighting to support was in fact economically sound, then economic factors may have motivated slaveholders more than the cultural issues that historians had previously assumed. A second conclusion was that slavery allegedly did not do as much damage to the slave family as believed because slaves were treated as though the family was an economic unit. Fogel and Engerman also claimed that whereas slaves were treated in a despicable manner physically, they were treated no worse than other social groups. For instance, their diet was higher in calories than Northern white workers, and their life expectancy was similar to free white workers in some areas. Their life expectancy was slightly lower than for Northern whites but the same as free white workers in Europe and higher than industrial workers in the North.

These sorts of conclusions, whatever their merits, are made possible by quantifying evidence on slavery and using the aggregate numbers as a standard instead of the impressionistic evidence of individual accounts. The controversial aspect of the book, of course, was that it seemed to advocate a rehabilitation of slavery, and certainly it failed to consider the moral dimension of the problem. The power of their "facts" thus blinded the authors to the moral aspect. The extreme distance between actual experience and the theoretical world of totally rational behavior within a logical market suggests that this heavily economic perspective may fail to encompass human reality.

Quantification provides an obvious methodology for questions of economics, demography, and crop production, but can it be applied to individual actions or even attitudes? Of what value is quantification in evaluating religious belief or political ideology as factors contributing to change? Michel Vovelle used quantification to estimate the degree of belief in southeastern France during the eighteenth century based on the weight of candles burned in churches.[3] What is the connection between religious beliefs and the size and number of candles burned at saints' altars? Vovelle was able to display the level of outward signs of religion, but the exact degree of religious piety at any time in history may be unknowable to historians.

Statistical methods have also been applied to textual studies. Scholars analyze words and rhetorical devices within a text and then compare the results to other texts. This type of analysis provides insights into authorship and the influence of related texts. The delineation of statistically significant corrections is part of a broader attempt to remove the observer from the analysis. The pursuit of more objective history based on statistics seeks to remove the historians' biases from the writing of history.

4.2 ECONOMICS AND HISTORY

Chapter 1 briefly explained Enlightenment notions of progress based on Comte's three teleological stages of history: a progression from a theological to a metaphysical and finally a positive stage. The positive stage of history attained knowledge through objective and precise analysis that was void of theological explanations in terms of God and metaphysical ones based on abstract thought. The positivists replaced God and abstract notions with objective and precise analysis. The positivist insistence on objective facts and quantifiable data produced a reliance on material analysis, that is to say, the study of tangible items such as wealth as opposed to abstract notions and ideas that are less easily measured. Yet Comte's initial three stages explained how an abstract idea or paradigm best defined an entire era.

Comte and Hegel had obvious differences, yet both espoused theories of historical progression within paradigms of thought and ideas. A similar phenomenon happened to Hegel's dialectical process, an ideological unfolding of history, when Marx revised it from ideas into a question of material, economic factors. Hegel's dialectical process explained history as an evolution of thought over time. He argued that a thesis dominated history until contested by its rival antithesis. The conflict between the thesis and antithesis forced the creation of a synthesis, which became the new thesis. Hegel's dialectical process worked through ideas that constitute the spirit of an age:

Thesis → Antithesis → Synthesis (new thesis)

Marx used Hegel's dialectical model but sought the spirit of the age in a society's material basis instead of its ideas. Dialectical materialism is based on the assumption that the motor of change is the development of society's productive arrangements:

Mode of production (thesis) → Opposing productive forces that emerge from within the system (antithesis) → New and more productive economy (synthesis)

The mode of production is the combination of the productive forces (units of production such as tools, materials, and workers) and the relations of production (relations that people establish during the process of production). For Marx, the relations of production remain static, but over time the productive forces evolve and pose a challenge to the mode of production. The result is a revolution where the original mode of production, or thesis, is replaced by a new mode of production (synthesis). Marx's dialectical materialism is therefore extremely teleological because

Marx knew how the modes of production had evolved and where they were headed. Marx posited five economic systems of modes of production through which society progresses:

Primitive community
Slave state
Feudal state
Capitalist system
Socialist society

The basic tenet of Marxist analysis is that the motor of change is the development of society's material basis, its productive arrangements. Change takes place in a society's means of production, which thus begin to come into conflict with the social arrangements built up on the basis of older forms of production. This tension eventually leads to revolution and the creation of a new regime.

Society is structured like a pyramid, and causal relations percolate upward:

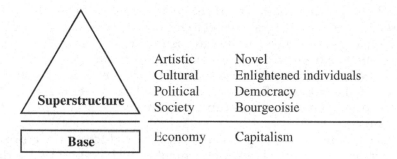

Superstructure	Artistic	Novel
	Cultural	Enlightened individuals
	Political	Democracy
	Society	Bourgeoisie
Base	Economy	Capitalism

The economy is the motor force of history. Economic change percolates upward and creates a new superstructure. The entire process is heavily deterministic: what takes place at lower levels determines what will happen higher up. Changes in the economic base of the pyramid necessitate changes in the superstructure above it.

The modes of production form an economic base upon which all other aspects of a society are hierarchically determined. History becomes the history of modes of production, and causation or change is explained in terms of economic determinism. Economic class becomes the central focal point of historical study because it is the main historical actor, or mechanism for historical progress, that moves history.

Economic class is based on shared relationships to the mode of production—namely, a group of people united by their position in production. Speakers of English are familiar with notions of economic class because English contains common terms such as "middle class" and "lower class." For Marx, people are united by their objective position in the hierarchy of production into various classes that tend to polarize into two oppositional classes such as the bourgeoisie (landowners who collect rents and capitalists who collect profits) and the proletariat (workers who create value by producing goods). Simply put, the bourgeois class gains income from rents and profits, whereas the proletariat gains income through labor.

Remarkably, Adam Smith and Karl Marx share a labor theory of value. But Smith and Marx disagree on how the newly created value should be distributed. Smith believes that a commodity is worth the amount of labor someone will give for it. Marx believes that a commodity is worth the socially necessary labor time required for production. The difference between the two theories of value has significant implications for profits. Smith believes that profits are just and fair because someone wanted to pay for the commodity. Marx argues that only labor creates new value but the capitalists take some of that value and call it profits. Thus capitalists and laborers will work harmoniously together for Smith because higher profits will allow the capitalist to pay workers more. Marx believes that even if real wages rise the relative wages of laborers shrink. Real wages are tied to the ability to purchase more while relative wages are wages relative to the profits, or "stolen" value, that capitalists take from workers. So even if purchasing power increases, relative wages decrease because the capitalist's profit is actually value created by the workers. For Marx, class relations under capitalism will always be antagonistic because capitalists are always stealing value from the laborers.

Class is determined by position in the productive structure, and each person has an objectively determinable position and thus a determinable class interest. There is thus a real, objectively determinable set of interests that corresponds to each class. Members of a class who do not agree with this interest (e.g., Catholic, working-class widows in Quebec who vote Conservative instead of Labor) thus are suffering from false consciousness—they have failed to understand their real situation. False consciousness occurs when people do not realize their class interest.

Definitions of class consciousness and false consciousness are central to distinguishing various forms of Marxists. "Vulgar" Marxists link the idea of class solely to the economy and argue, for instance, that American workers have false consciousness because of a myth of social mobility. Many historians find this view of class consciousness too deterministic and argue that Marx's goal was to provide a theory of how society changes instead of an accurate account of reality. Marx's focus on change instead of reality forced him to oversimplify class into two broad types in order to highlight causal arguments (Marx also discusses other classes or subgroups such as plebeians and petite bourgeoisie). From this perspective, Marx is somewhat ahistorical because he is not trying to describe what society looked like at a given time, but rather to work out the underlying logic of power struggles within society.

It is important to distinguish Marx's methodological decisions from his teleological assumptions. Marx's teleology explains change with clear assumptions about where society is heading: toward ever-greater freedom combined with superior technological sophistication. Just as capitalism triumphed over feudalism and brought more freedom and technological progress, so too communism will combine the fruits of capitalism and give humanity even more freedom. Marx's methodological decisions, however, need not be teleological. Historians can accept his method of analyzing the economic base of society and the way that class tensions move history without accepting a set political teleology.

Marx's methodology is noteworthy because his analysis of the French Revolution provided a significant break from prior interpretations. Marx can be seen as the first modern historian of the French Revolution because he posited that the Revolution destroyed feudalism and established new relations of production. One can accept Marx's analysis and then divorce his method and conclusions from his teleology by rejecting his theory that future revolutions are inevitable.

Not until Marx did we get any sort of recognizably modern interpretation of the French Revolution. The English conservative Edmund Burke could make no sense in his contemporary account of why the French Revolution came about. He constructed a conspiracy theory where upwardly mobile petty lawyers and doctors took action because they were, in effect, dissatisfied yuppies. Burke was unable to grasp the social situation and instead viewed the Revolution as the government's political bungling in response to minor discontentment. Thomas Carlyle offered another conspiracy theory from the opposite point of view: society was so corrupt that the French Revolution was inevitable. But he offered no reason for why this Revolution happened when it did. Jules Michelet, one of the first great writers of the French Revolution, explained it simply in terms of good versus evil, with the king representing evil and the Enlightenment philosophers representing good.

Marx viewed the French Revolution as vast social change based on economic developments before the Revolution. Prior to the Revolution, the feudal aristocratic regime developed the beginnings of trade and capitalism. These changes created a propertied bourgeoisie who became dissatisfied with their place in society. The Revolution therefore adjusted and realigned society, bringing these internal conflicts into harmony. The bourgeoisie, the capitalist class, could no longer exist under the system of feudal privilege and restrictions. The bourgeoisie created a capitalistic, free-market economic system and a fairly democratic political regime based on their interpretation of the Enlightenment philosophy of individuality, rationality, and progress. The Revolution stands as the endpoint of a long development of social and economic contradictions. These are the important factors; the Revolution itself is less crucial. Classes came into conflict with each other in the Revolution for objective and necessary reasons.

Marx's own assessment evolved as a result of the 1848–1850 European rebellions. In 1848, Marx and Engels confidently predicted in their *Communist Manifesto* that an inevitable and spontaneous revolution was imminent. Over the course of the next two years, Marx elaborated in *Class Struggles in France, 1848–1850* that the French proletariat would recover from its 1848 defeat and reconstruct itself as a class and a political party. He optimistically believed this reconstruction had taken place and that revolution would come quickly. This confidence diminished, and his 1852 book, *The Eighteenth Brumaire of Louis Bonaparte*, pessimistically examined why the spontaneous and inevitable revolution had not taken place. Marx's questions about the degree to which the revolution was spontaneous and inevitable are minuscule compared to later revisions such as those offered by Lenin. Currently, most revisionists challenge Marx's definition and use of class because they believe that people act for reasons more complicated than simple economic class.

Alfred Cobban's *The Social Interpretation of the French Revolution* offers a 1960s' revision of Marx's concept of class.[4] Cobban rejects Marx's theory of antagonism between two classes and revises it into a clash within the bourgeois class. He shows that some commoners owned land and acted like nobility while many aristocrats acted economically like capitalists; hence, Marx was wrong when he claimed that such actions could not happen because the bourgeoisie should all share the same class interest. His attack has led to a new focus for revisionists at the political level (for or against political change). Cobban argues that the Marxist conflicts between bourgeoisie and aristocracy and between feudalism and capitalism did not really exist, because revolutionaries and antirevolutionaries were of all social and economic positions. Many of the revolutionaries were aristocrats, and many who opposed the Revolution were bourgeois. Furthermore, the Revolution did not bring about the introduction of the capitalist system to France. Instead, the French Revolution came about because of antagonisms between prospering and declining members of the bourgeoisie (i.e., as the result of conflict within the bourgeoisie). Cobban therefore destroys the particular Marxist account of which groups were doing the fighting, but he still thinks that the actors were classes.

The result is a revisionist challenge to Marx's definition and use of class. Most revisionists see the Revolution as the outcome of struggles among members of the bourgeoisie and the aristocracy over the formation of a new bourgeois-noble elite. Whether one was for or against the Revolution had little to do with one's class position and was instead an ideological or political decision. The whole focus of the explanations has thus shifted to the political level: revisionist historians no longer look for the economic causes of these antagonisms, but see them as purely political. The most extreme of such historians deny that the concept of class makes sense. The result is a modification of Marxist concepts of class that has made them more flexible and useful.

4.3 SOCIOLOGY AND HISTORY

In the nineteenth century, the French philosopher Auguste Comte coined the term "sociology" and championed sociology as the "queen of the sciences." He held that it had the greatest opportunity to continue his teleological notion of human progress because sociologists could understand and therefore correct social evils. Subsequent sociologists have dropped Comte's teleology but still believe that the study of human tendencies can improve society.

As a field of study, sociology is a relatively new discipline. Sociology was not a university discipline at Cambridge University in 1949 when T. H. Marshall gave a series of lectures there entitled *Citizenship and Social Class*. Marshall opened by pointing out that Cambridge "has not yet accepted sociology as an inmate . . . It may be that sociology is on trial here in my person." Marshall's lectures combined historical, comparative, and sociological analysis into essentially a sociology of development. This approach was at odds with the more popular quantitative sociology of the 1950s. But by the mid-1960s, Marshall's combination of history and sociology into a sociology of development became very popular among both sociologists and historians.

Initially, the distinction between history and sociology was virtually nonexistent. Both fields have laid claim to the works of Montesquieu, Voltaire, Tocqueville, Marx, and Max Weber. Sociology began to focus on the present and to abandon analysis of the past at roughly the same time that anthropologists began to emphasize fieldwork. Emile Durkheim's 1897 study of suicide and Bronislaw Malinowski's emphasis on field studies in the early twentieth century were focused on the present. Anthropologists and sociologists were not limited by the fragmentary nature of historical records. Their theories of comparative and contrasting social conditions were most easily constructed with field studies and surveys of living people. In principle, Durkheimian sociology should be historical in order to delineate the conditions determining contemporary large-scale structures and forms of society, but Durkheim himself devoted little attention to comparisons of real historical societies. Durkheim relied largely on modern statistics and surveys to show the conditions for normal social integration and then contrasted that with suicide, a negative canvas, to offset the normal. He substituted contemporary field studies of tribal societies for the more difficult task of studying the history of a society. Field studies of living individuals provide many advantages over the analysis of historical fragments, but this line of research also requires naive faith in linear evolution.

Twentieth-century functionalist and neofunctionalist sociologists, such as Talcott Parsons and his followers, see little role for history. At the same time, the field of historical sociology has developed a meaningful challenge to the presentist focus of sociology. The methodological assumptions of history and sociology are not always in agreement. Historians are threatened by the sociological focus on regularities and law-like statements, whereas sociologists see historians as seeking to hide theory behind empirical facts. Since some degree of theory is unavoidable, why do historians refuse to be explicit about it? Why do historians refuse to face the fact that historical investigations are based on a range of theoretical assumptions?

Most historians obfuscate the theory behind their work and rely on implicit theory instead of explicitly formulated theory. Historians and sociologists are separated not by the lack or presence of theory, but rather by their respective rhetorics. Historians use a rhetoric of close presentation, whereas sociologists use a rhetoric of perspective. Sociologists have forced historians into an art-versus-science type of debate that centers on the role of generalizations versus particulars. Sociologists offer explicitly formulated theory as a framework for understanding reality, whereas historians examine reality and occasionally move to historically contingent theories. The following chart reveals this fundamental dichotomy between using theory as a perspective on reality versus using close presentation as a step toward theory:

The flow chart also reveals a second issue distinguishing historians and sociologists: the distinction between micro and macro analysis of an event. Historians tend to focus on the specific event, much like a scientist viewing an item through a microscope. Sociologists on the other hand tend to focus on broader events, much like a scientist viewing an item through a telescope. The tension between the micro and macro positions has been bridged by historical sociology: a broadening of history, new methods, and more flexible and historically contingent models. Both historians and sociologists made concessions in creating the field of historical sociology. Historians broadened the focus of history, accepted quantification, and embraced more explicitly theoretical approaches. Sociologists realized that high levels of abstraction can obfuscate, accepted that more information is needed, and embraced analysis of the past as a prerequisite for understanding problems. The resulting models are more flexible and frequently employ midlevel generalizations instead of overarching theories.

The best way to understand how this combination of history and sociology benefits the writing of history is to examine successful examples. For instance, Risto Alapuro's analysis of the 1918 revolution in Finland, *State and Revolution in Finland*, combines sociology and midlevel generalizations.[5] Alapuro makes the Finnish Revolution interesting to a broader audience by revealing the interaction between a small country, Finland, and a large country, Russia. He shows that external factors, such as relations with larger nations, are highly significant factors in explaining events in smaller nations. The Finnish Revolution was a different type of revolution than the Russian Revolution because of the role that Russia played in Finland. The collapse of Russian clientage power, combined with Russia's formal policies toward Finland, contributed directly to the Finnish Revolution. Alapuro still acknowledges the need to study internal factors and characteristics such as class when considering larger nations like Russia, but external factors offer a more viable causal explanation for the Finnish Revolution than internal class issues.

Theda Skocpol's *States and Social Revolutions: A Comparative Analysis of France, Russia, and China* compares revolutions in what Alapuro would consider large countries.[6] She argues that the state developed into an autonomous entity that became an independent actor in society and history. Her comparative analysis of revolutions focuses on the state instead of society and claims that the state is more than a reflection of social forces and the handmaiden of the strongest class. The resulting notion of some autonomy of the state poses a new thesis that has sparked intense responses.

Even more ambitious in scope is Perry Anderson's comprehensive description and analysis of the process by which Western Europe passed from the age of feudalism to that of absolutism in *Lineages of the Absolutist State*.[7] He examines virtually every major nation that seems to have undergone a change from an agricultural, feudal system to that of absolutism and capitalism between the thirteenth and nineteenth centuries. He points out particulars and commonalties in a manner that is quite different from the two methods previously employed by other Marxist historians—namely, abstract theorization about transition that ignored local differences and particular stories of social inequality that offered little about the general process and its worldwide ramifications. He concludes that absolutism in Western Europe cannot be considered an antiaristocratic system wherein kings actually achieved "absolute" authority for two reasons: (1) noble control of the economy and military existed under the new "ideological" terms of mercantilism, centralism, and bureaucratization; and (2) all monarchs were originally noble stock, and thus their end was always the furtherance of their power, and that of their class, at the expense of the toiling masses.

The transition from feudalism to absolutism-capitalism took place in the West not simply, nor even mainly, because of changes in the underlying modes of production and relations of the means of production. For Anderson, Western development should be seen as a very subtle process of growth, wherein each successive period contained many elements of its predecessors, no matter how "progressive" it seems to have been. Thus, absolutism was not a "novel" system, but a "concatenation" of classical, feudal, Renaissance, and "modern" aspects: "The actual movement of history is never a simple changeover from one pure mode of production to another: it is always composed of a complex series of social formations in which a number of modes of production are enmeshed together, under the dominance of one of them."[8] Anderson thus combined Marxist, cultural, and comparative analysis in a manner that addresses all three. His method involves an "organic" view, and his argument is in essence much like that of Johan Huizinga in his famous *The Waning of the Middle Ages*.[9]

Another example of ambitious comparative history is Barrington Moore's *Social Origins of Dictatorship and Democracy*.[10] Moore dispels unilinear theories of modernization and champions instead the theory that a variety of historically contingent routes to modernization are possible. He analyzes three specific routes to modernity: (1) bourgeois revolution via violence such as those of the middle classes of England and France, (2) a revolution from above after a middle-class revolution failed and authoritarian political structures remained such as occurred in Germany and Japan, and (3) Russian and Chinese communist revolutions that created modern economic and social forms but not political forms (absence of a middle class in Chinese trade).

All history is laden with theory. Alapuro, Skocpol, Anderson, and Moore are examples of how to combine midlevel generalizations with historical specificity. The combination of particularism and theoretical contextuality produces better empirical research and more fascinating theories. Theory and historical reality coalesce into a history informed by sociological theory and a sociology informed by historical specificity.

4.4 ANTHROPOLOGY AND HISTORY

In the early sixteenth century, Europeans experienced greater interaction with peoples from around the world. The encounters had a profound influence on European notions of otherness, slavery, and human nature in general. French philosopher Jean-Jacques Rousseau argued that the *noble savage*, or natural human, is fundamentally different from humans in contemporary society. In his 1755 book *Discourse on the Origin of Inequality*, Rousseau argued that European civilization has developed out of the gradual replacement of natural needs with artificial needs. The savage used instinct to fulfill needs, but changes took place as the savage's developing mind perverted the senses and created new passions: "The progress of the mind has been precisely proportionate to the needs received by peoples from nature or to those needs to which circumstances have subjected them, and consequently to the passions which inclined them to provide for those needs."[11] For Rousseau, natural needs are good and artificial needs are bad, because people become enslaved by the multitude of fresh needs. Natural needs bring equality and freedom, whereas artificial needs bring inequality and lack of freedom. It is the interaction between the number of needs and the acquisition of new techniques that drives the transition from the savage to the civilized person.

Functionalist anthropologists have expanded on Rousseau's notion of human needs transforming individuals and society. In the early twentieth century, the Polish-born British anthropologist Bronislaw Malinowski examined the social functions of customs and beliefs. He traced the biological foundations of values and saw culture as an answer to a list of needs. Malinowski attempted to explain how social practices fulfilled biological needs. He distinguished between basic needs and derived needs:

> By need, then, I understand the system of conditions in the human organism, in the cultural setting, and in the relation of both to the natural environment, which are sufficient and necessary for the survival of group and organism. A need, therefore, is the limiting set of facts. Habits and their motivations, the learned responses and the foundations of organization, must be so arranged as to allow the basic needs to be satisfied.[12]

Needs that fulfill the conditions necessary for individual and group survival are categorized as "basic needs." Culture takes on a biological survival value as the cultural satisfaction of basic needs results in new cultural needs that impose a secondary type of determinism. This secondary determinism is embodied in derived needs. Culture becomes a social structure that satisfies both the basic needs and the derived needs of the individual.

Malinowski emphasized the biological determinants of cultural actions because he wished to provide a perspective of analysis and comparison that was universally valid. Following his model, scholars could analyze and compare all societies at all times. Critics contend that it is inherent in his subject/object relation that the design of the culture originates from the anthropologist: "Rather than submit himself [the anthropologist] to the comprehension of a structure with an independent and authentic existence, he understands that structure by his comprehension of its purpose—and so makes its existence depend on him."[13] The functionalist therefore builds a diagram or system of cultural dynamics within which one can study the activities of others. Needs in all of their various forms are intensified interests that serve as the dynamic forces bringing the system into motion and leading it toward its functional end. By studying the activities or actual behavior of an individual within a human group, functional anthropologists hope to reach an understanding of the satisfaction of needs. This consideration of culture, as a group of patterned means for the fulfillment of needs, is based on two assumptions: (1) action occurs in answer to a need or want, and (2) these needs or wants exist in some form of hierarchy or list.

What roles can such a notion of needs play in historical analysis? The teleological character of the concept of needs causes theorists to camouflage, willingly or unwillingly, imperatives under the guise of an empirical base. The absence of a historicalization of needs presupposes a static human nature whereby needs are the cause of behavior. This presupposition demands the establishment of an empirical base that supersedes any values of its establisher. Until ethologists and sociobiologists provide such an empirical base, functionalist methodologies seem destined to be of little value to historians. And in fact, functional anthropology offered little in the way of methodological application to the study of the past until some currents in anthropology and history moved closer together and openly shared common methodologies in the 1970s. The resulting cross-fertilization has been fruitful but has also created certain healthy tensions. These tensions have forced historians to reconsider notions of human nature and timeless regularities.

Since the 1970s, Clifford Geertz has arguably been the anthropologist with the greatest influence on the study of history. His phrases "from the native's point of view" and "thick description" have made their way into a wide range of historical works. "Thick description" is essentially the interpretive analysis of culture modeled on semiotic explanation rather than the search for laws commonly found in experimental science. Geertz does straight anthropology based on field studies while creatively posing questions and utilizing methodology in a fashion of great interest to historians. Geertz's book *Negara: The Theatre State in Nineteenth Century Bali*, on the Balinese state, provides a substantive example of how anthropological studies of the state can influence the way historians approach history.[14] His analysis of how Bali maintains itself as a community, through rituals and public spectacles, even after a king dies poses daunting issues for historical studies of what a state is and what states do. The nineteenth-century Balinese state had little to do with the concentration, brokering, and application of power. Apparently the Balinese state existed for reasons of pomp and circumstance that were incidental to most Western states.

Geertz posits a doctrine of the exemplary center as the justification of the Balinese state: it represented in its rituals the Balinese view of the universe. The state was not the focus of power as it is in Western states with their utilization of ceremony, pomp, and spectacle; instead, the power served the pomp in Bali. *Negara*, the Balinese term for state or realm, was a microcosm of the cosmology and was therefore representative of how the Balinese saw the universe. Ritual and public spectacle take on a different role in this society, thereby forcing scholars to reconsider the provincialism of their assumptions about the state and power. Geertz successfully takes the ritual seriously but fails to show whether the interpretation is consistent with how the people themselves see it. If historians took Louis XIV's court or Hitler's Nuremberg rallies as a mirror of culture, would either of these provide the best "reading" of the society or simply one of many possible readings?

When applied to the past, anthropology can bring a sensibility of the otherness of the past that is frequently overlooked by historians. For instance, Emmanuel Le Roy Ladurie's *Montaillou* reconstructs southern French village life in the Middle Ages based on extensive Inquisition records.[15] Catharism was rampant in the region, and the Inquisition examined a broad range of everyday issues to ferret out the Cathar heresies. The result is a unique record that Le Roy Ladurie analyzed much like an anthropological record to reconstruct everyday life. He assumes that his subjects have little in common with us and that we will be interested in the details of everyday life. He analyzes the egalitarian peasant society and looks at how beliefs spread from one household, the basic unit of the society, to another household. He also provides a glimpse of such aspects of daily life as hygiene and sex. The work is highly successful in explaining these issues but fails on broader issues such as the notion of childhood. Despite the considerable charm of *Montaillou*, one problem with the book is that one does not actually learn much from it in a broader sense. But, certainly students of history enjoy reading something that has such charm whether they learn in a broader sense or not.

Some of the most successful cross-fertilizations between history and anthropology have been historical accounts constructed with a reference to anthropological comparisons. For instance, Keith Thomas's *Religion and the Decline of Magic* compares early modern Europe with tribes and peoples studied by anthropologists.[16] He modifies anthropologists' theories about the role of wizards in solving crimes, and applies them to European history. Wizards purportedly announce the person that the victim most suspects and thereby force the onus of solving the case on that person. The accused must prove his or her innocence by uncovering what happened. Thomas's work poses two key issues: (1) the existence of beliefs in magic because people had little control over their environment, and (2) the competition between magic and religion to bring the natural order under human control. The result was a process of desacralization where the church adopted the idea of miracles from pagan beliefs in order to compete with them. Magic was used when humans could not control their environment, such as with the weather, but not with things they could control such as the actual sowing of seeds. The Protestant Reformation attacked this mixture of religion and magic. The result was that the two became distinguished from one another at the same time that humans gained more control over crops due to technology. But Thomas goes further and rejects Malinowski's idea because more technology created further problems of insecurity.

Anthropological comparisons inspired Thomas to consider new perspectives, but there are also many references to other peoples that do not shed much light on the European past. The same goes for *Montaillou*. The problem is that some of the causal connections are simply too weak. Anthropological history often finds similarities and draws parallels but does not always show causal connections between the past and the present. If such connections exist because of inherent traits of human nature, then a more viable theoretical model would be that of psychohistory, which we will examine later in this book. The basic difference between history and these related disciplines is that historians reject some parallels that anthropologists and sociologists hold dear. The timeless regularities and generalizations of some anthropologists and sociologists are not consistent with historians' assumptions that the past should be understood in its peculiarity. Overall, the cross-pollination of history has been remarkably positive: historians have been forced to consider the methodological implications of their work in a manner that has prevented them from becoming too smug in their interpretations of the past.

NOTES

1. Section headings from the 1972 English edition of Fernand Braudel's *The Mediterranean and the Mediterranean World in the Age of Philip II* (New York: Harper & Row, 1972) reveal the use of economic models: Part Two—"Collective Destinies and General Trends"; Chapter 1—"Economies: The Measure of the Century"; Section 3—"Is It Possible to Construct a Model of the Mediterranean Economy?" pp. 418–461.

2.   Robert William Fogel and Stanley L. Engerman, *Time on the Cross: The Economics of American Negro Slavery* (Boston: Little, Brown, 1974). See also Fogel and Engerman's *Time on the Cross: Evidence and Methods, a Supplement* (Boston: Little, Brown, 1974).

3.   Michel Vovelle, *Piété baroque et déchristianisation en Provence au XVIIIe Siècle: Les attitudes devant la mort d'après les clauses des testaments* (Paris: Plon, 1997). An abridged version was published in 1997 by Editions du C.T.H.S.

4.   Alfred Cobban's 1962 "Wiles Lectures" were published two years later as *The Social Interpretation of the French Revolution* (Cambridge: Cambridge University Press, 1964).

5.   Risto Alapuro, *State and Revolution in Finland* (Berkeley: University of California Press, 1988).

6.   Theda Skocpol, *States and Social Revolutions: A Comparative Analysis of France, Russia, and China* (New York: Cambridge University Press, 1979).

7.   Perry Anderson, *Lineages of the Absolutist State* (London: N.L.B., 1974).

8.   Ibid., p. 423.

9.   Johan Huizinga, *The Waning of the Middle Ages* (Harmondsworth: Penguin Books, 1976).

10.   Barrington Moore, Jr., *Social Origins of Dictatorship and Democracy: Lord and Peasant in the Making of the Modern World* (Harmondsworth: Penguin Books, 1969).

11.   Jean-Jacques Rousseau, "*Discourse on the Origin of Inequality*"; in *On the Social Contract and Discourses*, trans. Donald A. Cress (Indianapolis: Hackett, 1983), p. 126.

12.   Bronislaw Malinowski, *A Scientific Theory of Culture* (Chapel Hill: University of North Carolina Press, 1944), p. 90.

13.   Marshall David Sahlins, *Culture and Practical Reason* (Chicago: University of Chicago Press, 1976), p. 75.

14.   Clifford Geertz, *Negara: The Theatre State in Nineteenth Century Bali* (Princeton, NJ: Princeton University Press, 1980).

15.   Emmanuel Le Roy Ladurie, *Montaillou: The Promised Land of Error* (New York: Vintage Books, 1979).

16.   Keith Thomas, *Religion and the Decline of Magic* (London: Penguin, 1991). Originally published in 1971 in New York by Scribner.

Chapter 5

Varieties of History

On your way home from the restaurant, you encounter a group of fellow students who are majoring in a wide range of subjects. After briefly explaining the history of your roommate's disappearance, you politely listen to each person's explanation of the situation. You are stunned at the wide variety of accounts. Each interpretation offers a different focal point for evaluation: (1) the stress of university life that can only be understood within the context of the medieval origin of universities and the establishment of your college two hundred years ago; (2) the unique situation of lowly history undergraduates at your college; (3) tiny aspects of your roommate's idiosyncratic behavior in the recent past; (4) billions of years of evolutionary biology and geology, which have influenced the current situation; (5) philosophical links that exist between all students who have dropped out thus far this semester; (6) the cultural climate that causes students to leave school; (7) subconscious desires of your roommate based on doodling left on the bathroom wall; and (8) a comparative analysis of your roommate and a dropout at another university. The eight approaches are oversimplifications of eight varieties of history (1) big history, (2) history from the bottom, (3) microhistory, (4) macrohistory, (5) intellectual history, (6) cultural history, (7) psychohistory, and (8) comparative history. These eight varieties of history were all prevalent in the latter half of the twentieth century, yet they would have been considered suspect by most historians just one century ago.

Chapter 1 showed that the breakthrough to modern history began when Leopold von Ranke rejected teleology and sought to understand what actually happened (*wie es eigentlich gewesen*). Nineteenth-century historicism sought to understand the past on its own terms, whereas twentieth-century discussions of historicism and presentism suggested that it is impossible to fully remove the spectacles of the present. More significantly, the historical revolution of the twentieth century broadened the scope of history beyond Ranke's presentist focus on nation and state (remember that Ranke experienced the heightened nationalism of German unification and Italian unification). The new histories were grounded in a Rankean foundation, but they also modified the main tenets of Rankean history: (1) the hermeneutic focus on documents widened to include virtually anything from geology to meteorology; (2) the scope broadened to such an extent that what previously would have been a minor footnote became the topic of entire monographs; and (3) proponents of the historicist perspective began to acknowledge the inherent presentism of historical accounts.

The eight approaches to history (big history, history from the bottom, microhistory, macrohistory, intellectual history, cultural history, psychohistory, and comparative history) all share a concern for the past, but do they share anything other than that concern for the past? More importantly, are the approaches all equally valid, or are some better than others? If some are superior, then what criteria are necessary to ascertain the superiority? If all approaches are equally valid, then is history becoming ever more chaotic and less coherent as each new method is added as an accretion to the others?

5.1 SOCIAL HISTORY

5.1.1 Big History: Annales

"Big science" is done on a large scale with many researchers, lots of money, and grandiose equipment like particle accelerators. Big history is to history what big science is to science, and the French Annales tradition is the best example of big history. Initially, the Annales historians pursued history on a vast scale that shattered the Rankean focus on nation-states and offered instead a virtually limitless scope. Generous government subsidies in France and England allowed teams of researchers to quantify everything from population trends and crop productivity to tax collections and economic development. Despite the broader scope, the "big history" tradition was still profoundly historicist.

Fernand Braudel offered a plea for the unification of the social sciences in his 1958 article in the "Débats et combats" forum of *Annales*.[1] In this platform for social scientists, he argued that a necessary goal of historical study should include a historical recognition of *la longue durée* (long periods of structural and geographic time). *Histoire et durées* are to be approached through cyclic oscillations such as the reality of the climb and fall of long-term price cycles. This search for rhythms of time, even of very long durations, is in opposition to the *histoire événementielle* (history of events) that was prevalent in France prior to the Annales. *Structure* dominates the problem of the long duration in a move that marks a shift away from the Annales researchers' earlier interest in the history of mentalities. Structures are obstacles that limit or stop humankind, such as geographic limits and climate. The Annales placed the history of human events into the context of diverse structural factors.

Braudel viewed history as the sum of all possible histories: a collection of points of view about yesterday, today, and tomorrow. In order to avoid the choice of one history at the exclusion of another, he proposed that historians should define a hierarchy of forces or movements and then recast a constellation of them together. A mathematical analysis of history is made possible by reducing events to comparable units. Historians who use broad models can therefore apply regional studies to a wider historical totality. Braudel clearly meant that these models are not to be seen as predetermined laws in the way that some Marxist historians use them. Sociologists are closer to the dialectic of the long duration, whereas historians tend to move beyond merely discussing movements and seek to pinpoint the precise duration of movements. Braudel advocated the incorporation of all branches of the social sciences into a historian's study, because he was interested in movements for the entire length of the duration and for all categories of the social sciences. For Braudel, then, economic conjuncture and social conjuncture are facets of cyclic oscillations, and it is structure that dominates the problems of the long duration.

Three conflicting nineteenth-century traditions influenced the early Annales: (1) the scientific approach of the positivist's nomological model, (2) the historicism of Rankean hermeneutics, and (3) the dialectical, materialistic perspective of Marx and Engels. The nomological approach's logic of scientific inquiry had an obvious influence on the Annales employment of statistics. The hermeneutic rejection of all generalizations is embodied in the middle-of-the-road Annales stance of neither accepting nor rejecting all generalizations. The wide range of topics and methods offered by the Annales historians became "a heaven-sent oasis on the path away from Stalino-Marxist historicism."[2]

The Rankean tradition was long rejected by positivists in France prior to the Annales.[3] Ranke's theory of knowledge appeared unscientific and irrational to French positivists who presupposed that statements were capable of intersubjective validation. At the end of the nineteenth century, French sociologist Emile Durkheim shifted the emphasis of studies from the individual to the collective. Durkheim, and later the Annales historian Marc Bloch, maintained that society is manifested in concrete forms that are observable to the outsider and thus the only way to understand the individual is to place the individual within the context of society. Written documents alone are no longer sufficient because they present events through the subjectivity of the observer. Bloch argued for the analysis of the material framework within which consciousness is expressed. His primary concern with the rise and decline of social structure resulted in a procedure that is descriptive instead of explanatory. Annales research shifted from Bloch's qualitative structural history to a quantitative history of conjunctures after World War II. Simultaneously, the establishment of the Sixth Section of the École Pratique des Hautes Études meant that the erstwhile provincial Annales group had a governmentally financed institution in the heart of Paris.

Fernand Braudel's thesis in 1949 signaled a shift from interest in the history of mentalities to an interest in structure. In the 1960s, the quantitative economic history prevalent in the 1950s was superseded by historical demography, or the statistical analysis of population in history. These demographic studies frequently attempted to provide an explanation of the everyday life of the masses, as is evident in Le Roy Ladurie's *The Peasants of Languedoc*.[4] In going beyond this work to later works by Le Roy Ladurie, and the Annales in general, there is a strong shift back to the history of mentalities similar to the type that characterized the early Annales.

5.1.1.1 EARLY ANNALES

Early Annales historians like Lucien Febvre and Marc Bloch developed in the provinces far from the Parisian intellectuals. But shortly after World War II they had so captivated the Parisian universities that their journal became the premier historical journal in French-speaking lands. Bloch's bold analysis in *Feudal Society* and Febvre's *The Problem of Unbelief in the Sixteenth Century*[5] bespeak the initial interest in medieval and early modern history, but their scope was not limited to a specific time period. The title of the Annales' journal changed in 1946 from *Annales d'histoire économique et social* (Annals of Economic and Social History) to *Annales: Economies, Sociétés, Civilisations* (Annals: Economies, Societies, Civilizations). Both titles display a conscious attempt to marginalize political history, and the post-1946 subtitle more accurately reveals the broad scope and interdisciplinary appeal of the Annales. An editorial in the January–February 1994 issue announced a further change in the subtitle to *Annales: Histoire, Sciences Sociales*. The newest subtitle reflects growing discontentment with the focus on conjunctures and a willingness to view society and culture within the context of politics.

The Annales pursued a total history (*Sciences humaines*) that was problem oriented instead of fixated on facts. This is not to say that the works were not factual—they were—but the goal was to solve issues instead of posing mere facts. Historians of what Nietzsche called the Antiquarian tradition focused on collecting facts the way that stamp collectors gather stamps. The Annales historians only wanted facts that solved a problem. Febvre, for example, pursued the question of Rabelais's belief or agnosticism in *The Problem of Unbelief in the Sixteenth Century*.

The study was much more than a question of whether or not Rabelais was an agnostic; namely, was it possible for anyone to be an agnostic in sixteenth-century Europe? Febvre began with a problem about the spectrum of possible beliefs and looked to the past to solve it.

The Annales resisted the contemporary trend of specialization whereby history was chopped into distinct sectors such as social, economic, and political history. They moved in the opposite direction and broadened the scope and understanding of history as a whole much as Wagner's "Gesamtkunstwerk" had championed the opera as the total art form that would ultimately encompass all other art.

The early Annales mounted the first sustained attack on Rankean history (Karl Lamprecht's attack was short-lived before being revived in the 1970s by social historians) with their cross-fertilization of the social sciences under the guide of history. The premier social science became a history that (1) was problem oriented, (2) was not limited to national field or specific period, (3) incorporated many disciplines instead of relying on one specialization, and (4) attempted to be scientific once again.

The institutional structure of the Annales school was highly successful in part because generous government grants allowed large teams of scholars to work on grand projects. The hierarchical academic structures of French academia allowed individual scholars to employ teams to quantify a range of issues such as the demographic, economic, and domestic life of sixteenth-century Florence or the salaries and eating patterns of soldiers from the French Revolution. These teams compiled rich bases of source material for later scholars by combining this information with other quantifiable fields such as historical geography's data on crop distributions, field sizes, and ownership patterns. The first and second generation of Annales researchers were steeped in Rankean history and used this as a backdrop for their studies. The third generation, however, lacks a strong background in political history and as a result frequently examines more creative but also more specialized questions, as Alain Corbin did in his 1982 book exploring the history of fragrance. Historians outside the Annales tradition recognize the value of Braudel's massive work on the Mediterranean, with its obvious implications for a recognition of Philip II's achievements, but they have been less accepting of recent Annales works.

5.1.1.2 BRAUDEL AND ANNALES METHODOLOGY

Perhaps the best way to grasp the Annales is to examine Braudel's methodology. He posits a trinity of time:

1. *histoire événementielle* (events and individual time)
2. *conjuncture* (social time of intermediate duration), and
3. the *longue durée* (structural and geographic time).

Traditional history examines human events that fit into the *histoire événementielle* framework. These mere events, or actions of individuals and groups, would include the usual things that constitute normal history and life such as marriages, revolutions, and politics. The conjunctures of social time cover movements spanning several lifetimes such as the rise of industrialization. This intermediate duration is modeled on the study of economic patterns and demographic cycles such as Ernst Labrousse's study of grain prices. Last, Braudel pursued the *longue durée* that formed the bedrock of historical reality. These structures are best measured in geographical time and allow for analysis of geographical and climatic histories. Of Braudel's trinity of time, the *longue durée* required historians to make the most drastic adjustment because this kind of history changes at a pace far slower than traditional topics of history.

Braudel's work is based on a hierarchy of historical reality with a material base that parallels Marxist analysis, but Braudel is part of a structuralist movement that differs greatly from Marx. Braudel is more materialist because he looks at structures that are deeper than Marx's economic base. This deeper materialism looks not at people but at structures that change slowly over centuries of time. This depth creates vague notions of causality, whereas Marx's causality is a clear percolating of change from the economic base upward to the superstructure. Braudel is part of a broader movement within the social sciences that pursued more fundamental explanations. The linguist Noam Chomsky studied commonalities about language in pursuit of universal linguistic laws just as anthropologist Claude Lévi-Strauss compared human proclivities regarding incest in pursuit of universal laws of kinship. Braudel does not seek general laws, but the physical reality of the Mediterranean area provided a structure for historical reality. The connections between the three levels are vague because geographical determinism is much cruder than the causal arguments that one can derive from Marxist economic determinism. For instance, Braudel shows that life in the mountains is difficult because one is isolated and the climate is cold; hence, civilization occurred on the plains. Because it is harder to get to the mountains, it is also harder for the power of political authorities to penetrate the mountains; hence, the mountains are a frontier person's paradise because they allow more freedom. Braudel offers wonderful examples, but is this common sense, and are the causal links viable? Does Braudel show how things actually changed?

Braudel's two-volume study *The Mediterranean and the Mediterranean World in the Age of Philip II*[6] consists of three sections, beginning with the role of the environment and physical geography (*longue durée* of long-term structures), followed by the collective destiny and general economic and demographic trends (*conjuncture* of intermediate duration), and concluding with the military struggles between Spain and the Turks in a traditional history of the events, politics, and people of the Mediterranean (*histoire événementielle* of individual time). The phenomenal scope is evidence of the thirty years of research that went into a book originally intended to examine Philip II and his Mediterranean policies. Febvre suggested to Braudel that he reverse the traditional equation and write about the Mediterranean as a context for understanding Philip II. Despite the gigantic scope, the work is not a total history, but such an entity may be neither possible nor valuable. The question of valuable history returns us to Febvre's emphasis on problem-oriented history, something Braudel's study lacks unless one views the entire Mediterranean as a problem. Should history attempt to be problem oriented and total at the same time? Is it possible to show meaningful interrelations between the three layers of Braudel's time and simultaneously show how vital changes occurred?

Le Roy Ladurie's 1967 book on climate further developed the Annales tradition and revealed the extent to which it had expanded our sense of what can be history.[7] He incorporated studies of tree rings (dendochronology), harvest dates (phenology), and glaciers, just to mention three, into a history of a changing climate. The beauty of this study is in part its focus on a structure that is relevant to us; we can see how climate influences humans. Before "global warming" was an issue, this book explored the structural history of climate. The book also considered how climate, specifically the problem of global warming, related to people. The result was a combination of Braudel's structural issues with Febvre's emphasis on problems and causal change.

The expanded scope of history forces historians to consider the appropriate focus of a study. If the focus is too wide it becomes meaningless to human activity and if the focus is too narrow it becomes meaningless to other humans. Prior to the Annales, historians sought focal points between the hermeneutics of Ranke, with its emphasis on finding the unique in every event, and the scientific scope of Buckle's vast generalizations. Reactions to the Annales have profoundly shaped the study of history. One side has pushed for a narrower focus, a view through the microscope if you will, and another group has sought for a wider, or telescopic, focus. This split between microscopic and telescopic studies is evident in the emerging fields of macrohistory and microhistory.

5.1.2 Little History: History from the Bottom

History from the bottom is history written from the perspective of the masses, lower classes, and groups outside of the mainstream; it is not a history of the bottom. Like the Annales movement, history from the bottom is a clear reaction to the nineteenth-century focus on politics and the elites. Historians within the movement drew from and modified Annales methodology in an effort to widen the scope of history. David Sabean's delightful book *Power in the Blood: Popular Culture and Village Discourse in Early Modern Germany* offers an example of history from the bottom by providing six episodic studies of peasant life ranging from the 1580s until the 1790s.[8] Within each vignette, readers come to know individual peasants by name, yet the various dukes are never mentioned by name. The result is an about-face from a Rankean tradition that turned dukes and other elites into recognizable personalities but described any peasants as simple peasants. Sabean reverses this tradition by lumping the various dukes over the two-hundred-year period into "the duke" but giving individual peasants recognizable personalities. Much as students at a large state university may call the chancellor simply "the chancellor" (without identifying the actual person holding the position) and refer to individual students by name, *Power in the Blood* records the names of peasants but not the elite. Having made his point, Sabean does include the names and personalities of individual peasants and elites in his later works. *Power in the Blood* was an important exercise because, once written, it allows historians to return to more balanced approaches that recognize the personalities of the elites and the common peasants.

Sabean's analysis of kinship and power relations in rural Germany is representative of German *Alltagsgeschichte*, or the history of everyday life, but differs from other forms of history from the bottom. These differences are frequently related to national history; namely, German *Alltagsgeschichte* differs from Italian microhistory, English social history, and late Annales French social history. Beyond the national differences, a wide variety of methods have been used in writing history from the bottom. For instance, the early *Alltagsgeschichte* historians mixed history with social anthropology and focused on questions related to protoindustrialization. For political and national reasons, they and other "history from the bottom" historians have taken Annales history and modified it into a wide variety of histories.

Despite its debt to the Annales, history from the bottom was foreshadowed in a number of nineteenth-century works that focused on lower classes within one nation, such as Macaulay's study of English lifestyles in *The History of England* and Jules Michelet's study of "the common people," or *le peuple*.[9] The greatest proponent of this approach was Karl Lamprecht, a German historian who broke with Ranke's focus on the "great man" and strove instead to write a collective history based on all of society. Lamprecht was largely ignored until he was rediscovered and championed in the 1970s when historians began seeking a tradition of history from the bottom that was not as deterministic as Engels's famous study of the 1525 Peasants' War in German-speaking lands (*The Peasants' War in Germany*) and his study *The Condition of the Working Class in England*.

Social historians of the 1960s and 1970s shifted the focus from social elites to the inarticulate masses who were largely unimportant in previous histories. Many of them used Marxist presuppositions to construct histories of the working classes. This group tended to focus on the ideology of the working class, especially in the industrial period— for example, E. P. Thompson's efforts to rescue workers from the ridicule of being depicted as misguided utopians.[10] Saving workers from condescension was easily achieved in histories of the industrial period, but frequently other histories focused solely on revolutions such as the French Revolution and the Paris Commune. Uprisings were presented as a product of mobs or of a specific class, because those who actually protested, fought, and died were from the lower class. Social historians might seek, for instance, the seeds of industrial proletarian ideas among the sansculottes instead of relegating them to a simple mob mentality. A clear divide evolved with one camp of historians describing strikers as riffraff, instead of upright artisan-citizens, while another camp of historians defended their integrity as early precursors to the full-fledged urban proletariat. The point quite simply is that the study of history from the bottom was initially contingent on the historian's own political proclivities.

Beyond the political question, the democratization of historical interest to include groups other than the elites raised new methodological issues. The study of everyday lives and customs of individuals previously forgotten from history, or dismissed as insignificant, evolved from an anthropological interest in documenting these groups into a democratization of all subjects. The history of the bottom became important because of the bottom's significant role in historical events and not simply because of a voyeuristic interest in its uniqueness. The forgotten peoples became historical actors in their own right, and any attempt at recounting the past needed to take them into account. For instance, Georges Lefebvre established the role of the peasants in the French Revolution. Prior studies had explained a change of power from the societal elite to the middle class with little consideration for the peasants. Traditional Marxists saw the French Revolution as the moment at which the feudal system came into crisis and resulted in a rising of the middle class; hence, they focused on the urban bourgeoisie with little interest in the peasants.

Lefebvre's *Great Fear of 1789* showed that the peasants were active and had a political agenda.[11] The peasant revolts influenced the political negotiations in Paris because they forced the hands of the deputies, who had to institute quicker and broader reforms. The peasants faced harsh economic conditions that were made more acute by reforms such as those influencing grain prices. The ensuing epidemic of beggary in the countryside led to widespread peasant fear of an aristocratic conspiracy in Paris, and the peasants turned against the aristocrats and burned their records. After the great revolt, the peasants withdrew from politics, but Lefebvre's work shows their influence on revolutionary politics. The peasants were political actors, much like the sansculottes, the middle class, and the aristocrats, and their desire for reform provoked revolts that created further reforms.

George Rudé's *The Crowd in the French Revolution* focuses similarly on the role of the sansculottes and the crowd that stormed the Bastille.[12] The storming of the Bastille was an important event in the Revolution, but what exactly did the crowd want? The urban sansculottes differed from the middle class (bourgeoisie) on a range of interests such as the desire, shared with the peasants, to stabilize grain prices. The "history from the bottom" approach offers a fresh dimension to the French Revolution because it emphasizes new historical actors such as the sansculottes and the peasants. Historians heatedly contest the various interpretations of the French Revolution, but there exists a general consensus that history from the bottom has provided a more complete understanding while offering few disadvantages.

History from the bottom has been more controversial in other areas of history such as the Nazi period and the Holocaust. Historians traditionally presented the Nazi period in terms of high politics and diplomacy. The historical interpretations were contested and debated, but the degree of contention was small relative to the wide reactions to the new questions posed from the bottom such as why the average person would follow Hitler and how the Holocaust could possibly occur. Abstractions from simple reasoning, like the theory that economic depression frightened the average German into following Hitler, have been undermined by extensive studies of everyday life such as William Allen's *The Nazi Seizure of Power*.[13] Allen reconstructed a town's experience to show why the Nazis were popular. Surprisingly the central issue was not a question of losing one's job because most people in that town were civil servants with no cause for concern over unemployment. Instead, the Nazi leaders are defined as adept tacticians whose rallies and propaganda were entertaining and enjoyable. The manipulation, according to Allen, was not an issue of anti-Semitism because the Germans tended to vote for the party despite the party's anti-Semitism (most were largely indifferent to anti-Semitism).

Daniel Goldhagen, however, argues in *Hitler's Willing Executioners: Ordinary Germans and the Holocaust* that Germany alone was driven by a latent "eliminationist anti-Semitism" that imbued "ordinary Germans" with the belief that mass murder was justified.[14] Most historians have focused on the victims or grappled with the elite's construction of the machinery and policy of destruction, but, as the book's subtitle suggests, Goldhagen examines the Holocaust from the perspective of the ordinary citizens who actually acted against the Jews. The dehumanized killing machine is replaced by average Germans whose complicity is attributed to a cultural phenomenon of anti-Semitism that was markedly "eliminationist." The book has been heatedly debated inside and outside of Germany, and future histories will need to address Goldhagen's thesis because while Goldhagen examined specifics he never lost sight of a whole. He studied the trees and still told us about the forest.

One danger of history from the bottom is that the examination of specifics occasionally fails to address the whole. For instance, the creation of a new chronological timeline necessary to fit the everyday-life occurrences would emphasize what people experienced, but it might fail to recognize important aspects of high politics, especially those that contemporaries did not perceive as significant. The timeline might include unemployment rates in Munich, but would it include political negotiations in Munich? A further distortion of historical understanding is the quest for specifics that fails to recognize the whole. For instance, a study of issues opposite to Goldhagen's complicity could focus on resistance, or lack thereof, to the Nazi regime. History from the bottom that seeks resistance will obviously find it, but to what extent do such studies redefine and categorize other behavior as resistance? Granted, in a totalitarian regime it is necessary to redefine resistance because the regime does not allow visible resistance such as public protests, but to what extent is nonconformity in everyday actions actual resistance?

Detlev Peukert's examination of adolescent behavior revealed groups that were antagonistic to the regime such as the Hamburg circle of "Swing Kids" (also known as "Swings") that embraced jazz music.[15] But were these expressions of adolescent solidarity and nonconformity truly resistance? Young Germans were necessary for the Nazi regime, but many were inherently at odds with the regime. Was this intentional political resistance, or did the young people simply defy authority because young people tend to defy authority? Competent historians who seek evidence of covert resistance will usually be able to find it, but critics might claim that this study of the trees fails to reveal much about the forest.

5.1.3 Macrohistory

Macrohistory always recognizes the broader picture (forest) and avoids focusing on the events of individuals (the trees). Theories, or broad general concepts, are used by all historians who seek to make sense of the particulars. Macrohistory redefines the role of theory and the use of particulars for the study of history. It may be helpful to think of the differences between traditional history and macrohistory as similar to the difference between a scientist working on a specific experiment and a scientist working on a new explanatory theory. For instance, astronomers in 1500 were studying the motion of individual planets and stars while Copernicus was contemplating a new way of explaining the motion of the entire heavens. Copernicus dispelled the Ptolemaic system of astronomy by suggesting that the planets rotate around the sun. Copernicus's heliocentric, or sun-centered, theory of the heavens was achieved by rethinking the entire scope of astronomy. Macrohistorians are to traditional historians what Copernicus was to his contemporaries.

The scope of macrohistory is potentially limitless. It may be best to view the scope as a continuum of possible histories ranging from the history of infinity to simple comparative history. The two ends of the continuum would consist of (1) "Big History" macrohistorians who explore history from the origins of the universe clear into the future, and (2) macrohistorical sociologists who offer a world-historical perspective to traditional historical sociology (see Section 4.3). Both extremes revere Fernand Braudel and William H. McNeill as early examples of the contemporary macrohistory movement. Macrohistory is not new, but Braudel (in the 1950s) and McNeill (in the 1960s) started a twentieth-century revival that has gained in popularity with the end of the Cold War.

Post–Cold War changes in undergraduate curriculums have included a shift from Western civilization courses toward world civilization courses. This, combined with contemporary globalization in general, has contributed to an interest in how one area might be influenced by developments in areas far removed from it. Whereas national and regional historians tend to attribute change to factors inside of a specific nation or region, macrohistorians seek causal arguments that include the role of factors external to a region. The interest in "causality from the outside in" and the broad focus on global issues are two of the defining characteristics of contemporary macrohistory.

The broad theoretical scope of contemporary macrohistory has led some historians to contend that macrohistory is simply historical sociology with a stronger dose of sociology than history. The book *Macrohistory and Macrohistorians: Perspectives on Individual, Social, and Civilizational Change* "grew out of a seminar on social theory" held in the sociology department at the University of Hawaii at Honolulu. The authors contend that "macrohistory is the study of a unit through time (*diachronic*) and the study of noncontiguous points, neighborhoods and contexts. Macrohistory, then, surveys history across various units of analysis, searching for patterns, regularities, and change."[16] Traditional historical monographs provide data from which macrohistorians construct general theories of transformation. This pursuit of patterns and change aims not merely to understand the past, but to use that understanding of past structures to create new possibilities for the future.

"Macrohistory is ambitious, focused on the stages of history and the causes of change through time (*diachronic*). Macrohistory is not the study of some little region in space at the same point in time (*synchronic*)."[17] In Chapter 2, we described the differences between synchronic and diachronic history as analogous to the differences between a collage of photographs (*synchronic*) and a family photo album organized chronologically (*diachronic*). Synchronic historians focus on many aspects of a region in a fairly limited time frame. Macrohistorians employ an extremely broad diachronic scope that extends from the earliest of times clear on into the future. The focus on the future is far more pronounced than the presentism employed by most historians (see Chapter 3). Macrohistory has a strong following among a "future studies" movement that seeks to understand and improve the human condition.

David Christian opened a 1991 article with the argument that "the appropriate time scale for the study of history may be the whole of time. In other words, historians should be prepared to explore the past on many different time scales up to that of the universe itself—a time scale of between 10 and 20 billion years."[18] Christian has become the most visible advocate of "Big History" macrohistory that explores vast timescales. Moreover, he is one of the few theorists of macrohistory to also write macrohistory: his *Inner Eurasia from Prehistory to the Mongol Empire* was published by Blackwell in 1998 and his *Maps of Time: An Introduction to Big History* was published by the University of California Press in 2004. Thus far his works have been well received by teachers of world history but have had little influence beyond that group. His ambitious efforts have not won many historians to the billions-of-years scale for history but have allowed more traditional historians to consider the possibility of expanding the scale of history.

The other end of the macrohistorical timescale continuum has been quite well received by mainstream historians in the West. This side expands historical sociology to a macro-level and seeks world-history, instead of nation-state history, perspectives. Many historians find the broad scope of macrohistory daunting because they were professionally trained in one field within the study of history. The field-specific training of most historians makes it difficult for some historians to write, or even appreciate, a true macrohistory.

Sociologist Randall Collins looks at macrohistories that are more limited both in scope and in implications for the future than the "Big History" macrohistory of Christian. In the introduction to *Macrohistory: Essays in Sociology of the Long Run*, Collins credits William McNeill as the first professional historian to write modern macrohistory:

> McNeill's *The Rise of the West*, published in 1963, represents the maturity of world historiography, the point at which enough scholarship had accumulated so that the history of the globe could be written in conventional narrative form without resort to metaphor. In comparison with the

flamboyant efforts of the generation of pioneers, McNeill's world history is that of the professional historian, extending routine techniques and building on knowledge that had accumulated to the point where a world history was no longer a miraculous glimpse of a conjectured past.[19]

McNeill's delightful book, like many macrohistories, is aimed at students rather than at an audience of professional historians.

In the past decade, macrohistories written for an audience of professional historians have grown considerably in popularity. Most of these works look at questions of globalization and economic development. The significance of this recent development is evident in a number of historiographical overviews in *The American Historical Review* and panels discussing macrohistory at various conferences.[20] The narrower focus of these studies may remain unacceptable for the "Big History" macrohistorians. Macrohistory is here to stay, but it remains unclear whether the movement will come to embrace a narrower historical sociology tradition or remain tied to Christian's billions-of-years time frame.

5.1.4 Microhistory

History from the bottom democratized historical interest to include groups other than the elites. Initial attempts involved social historians quantitatively analyzing huge numbers of people. In the late 1970s, a group of Italian historians shifted the focus from quantitative analysis of groups to qualitative analysis of individuals from the "forgotten peoples" of history. Following the lead of social anthropologists, the practitioners of "microhistory" looked at utterances and beliefs of individuals as a conscious response to the immobile history of the *longue durée* (Annales). Their heuristic emphasis on the vestigial and the anomalous appealed to the subjective experience of individuals instead of quantitative generalizing. Dissatisfied with the macroscopic and quantitative model, they employed a circumscribed and close-up perspective modeled on Sherlock Holmes's attention to the most minute detail. Peter Burke aptly describes them as historians who "turned from the telescope to the microscope."[21]

Microhistory is a response to such dominant historical preoccupations as quantitative social science, the Marxist and structural-functionalist systems, immobile history, and the *longue durée*. The most famous practitioners of microhistory are the northern Italian historians Carlo Ginzburg and Giovanni Levi.[22] Both examine brief, dramatic events involving heretics in order to test the abstractions of social thought on specific individuals. Their most famous studies involve a fair amount of conjecture due to the relative paucity of source information about rural heretics and exorcists. Microhistorians look at a wide range of obscure evidence much as a tracker would look at seemingly unrelated clues to bring a hunting party to its prey. Their evidential paradigm is modeled loosely on the American pragmatist Charles Peirce's theory of abduction as a systematic method for sorting fragmented evidence into a meaningful paradigm. Peirce's abductive inferential process allows historians to draw inductive inferences that are at best probably true. Inductive arguments do not guarantee truths in the manner that deductive arguments do. Italian microhistorians combine this inductive pragmatism with an extreme nominalism that emphasizes the otherness of the past.

In a 1980s essay entitled "Clues: Roots of an Evidential Paradigm," Ginzburg theorized that historical narrative originated in a society of hunters. He claimed that narrative sprung from "the oldest act in the intellectual history of the human race: the hunter squatting on the ground, studying the tracks of his quarry."[23] Like a tracker on the hunt, the historian's minute investigation of trifling matters may allow individuals to understand what has happened and thus behave differently in the future. Historical narrative explains the past and in so doing foretells what might be done in the future. Microhistorians use focused microstudies of the past in order to draw general conclusions that are relevant to their contemporaries.

The "narrative" of microhistorians is not the same as that of traditional narrative history. Ginzburg explains that his own work is usually the product of serendipitous research; namely, while seeking one thing he chances upon a completely different conclusion that captures his attention. He then works "backward" from the solution to a fascinating question that was not initially evident. Like a tracker deciphering the traces of a previous hunt, Ginzburg's "evidential paradigm" allows him to work toward proving a hunch. This writing of history "backward" allows the historian to employ a new narrative device that is not bothered by gaps in the evidence. The facts do not lead Ginzburg to a conclusion; instead a hypothesis allows him to gather fragmentary evidence that supports his account. The final result is a new form of intellectual history that explores the shared presuppositions of common people. Microhistorians attempt to describe the trees and the forest based on microscopic analysis of a few pieces of bark.

5.2 INTELLECTUAL HISTORY

Intellectual historians assume that historical changes happen when ideas motivate people to take action; hence, intellectual historians emphasize ideas over material forces. This is not to say that material forces cannot act causally in history, but that ideas are a more significant motor of change. As a mode of writing, intellectual history traditionally explored how great books influenced one another. This "history of ideas" has since been expanded beyond the canonical texts of a few "great thinkers" and now includes virtually every aspect of human thought including popular opinions and irrational ideas. The move to a broader scope involved three transitions, or perhaps traditions in that all three remain with us today: (1) history of ideas, (2) contextualism, and (3) new intellectual history.

5.2.1 History of Ideas

The traditional history-of-ideas approach is evident in Arthur Lovejoy's *The Great Chain of Being*.[24] In the 1950s, Lovejoy traced the evolution of a "great chain of being" that was fundamental to Western thought from Plato through the nineteenth century. This study was not simply a history of philosophy that traced systems of thought; instead it focused on unit ideas. These unit ideas are purportedly traditional ideas of Western thought that are fundamental and remain constant. They can be broken apart and recombined, but in general we inherit them without exploring them. They fit within two attitudes or tendencies of human thought: to simplify into unified principles and to complicate by presenting the world in its complexity. An example of this type of thinking is Isaiah Berlin's adaptation of Archilochus's metaphor of the hedgehog and fox: the hedgehog uses one great idea to explain everything (like Hegel) whereas the fox employs many little ideas with no grand system (like the Enlightenment philosopher Voltaire).

The great chain of being is based on a mixture of Plato's principle of plenitude and Aristotle's notion of continuum. The principle of plenitude consists of a metaphysical belief that the creative force, call it God if you wish, manifested its perfection in our world. This creative force created the greatest possible number of beings because the manifestation of perfection means that it must have created everything that necessarily exists. The world then is more perfect if more things are in it. The abundant entities exist on a continuum whereby everything in the universe is arranged according to gradation or scale. The combination of plenitude and continuum constitutes the great chain of being, an extremely optimistic outlook on the world because all of the evils that do exist are necessary evils; without them the world would, in fact, be a worse place. All beings that could exist were created and all beings that do exist are on a continuum. Evil is necessary because without it this perfect world could not exist. The resulting "best possible world" view means that this world may not be the best theoretically conceivable world, but the best world possible because the creator would have created a better world if such a world were possible. The great chain of being contributes to the basic optimism of Western thought—the assumption that the world is, despite all nastiness, basically a good place.

This Western optimism differs from other world views such as the Manichean notion of a dichotomous universe with good struggling against evil. The fundamental pessimism of the Manichean view, or of other views that see the world as fundamentally evil, makes the Manichean and other views susceptible to a range of ideas that are unlikely to appear in the Western view.

The great chain of being ensures that the universe is the best possible world and that the abundance of variety is part of the goodness of the world. This interpretation shows the extent to which an idea is crucial to basic ideas of the universe. Humanity need not be the center of the universe, and we as individuals are not the center of anything. There is nothing particular about our planet and no great distinction between us and animals. We are part of nature and thus become concerned about the extinction of animals and the destruction of the rain forest. This idea also justifies a politics of affirmative action because we should not exclude different people. The Western idea helps make Copernicus's heliocentric theory, Darwin's evolutionary theories, and contemporary ecological theories plausible.

The great drawback with this definition of optimistic, Western uniqueness is that it is unclear that Lovejoy's rubrics apply to previous thinkers. One could argue, for instance, that Plato and Aristotle did not realize that they were talking about a great chain of being. In which case, the idea did not exist until Lovejoy constructed it.

5.2.2 The Contextualists

Do timeless truths really exist? The contextualist tradition of intellectual history rejects the assumption that timeless truths exist that need no context. The great books do not contain timeless truths that can be understood without consideration of their context because past thinkers were not talking about the same sorts of things throughout the evolution of an idea. Historians need to recreate the context surrounding an individual text. One reason for the different assumptions of the contextualists is that they tend to focus on political thought and ideology instead of the broader philosophical issues that are believed to be central by the proponents of the history of ideas.

The assumption that a grasp of context is integral to understanding a text makes the contextualists profoundly historicist. This extreme historicism leads them to reject the history-of-ideas focus as an indulgence in anachronism. They claim that the lack of context produces anachronisms and distortions because the historian is attempting to make the past fit into a prescribed theory. For instance, Quentin Skinner shows that Marsilius of Padua drew a theory of separation of power (legislative and judicial) whereby the ruler has executive power and the people have legislative power.[25] This apparent separation of powers should not be seen as part of the popular discussion of the separation of powers that occurred two centuries later. Skinner reconstructs the context of Marsilius's ideas in order to show that one should not see him as the originator of the separation-of-powers doctrine.

Contextualists believe that context is the supreme factor in analysis. Meaning is distorted if a work is not placed within the framework of what it meant when it was written. One rationalization for this reliance on context is evident in theories of speech acts put forward by John Austin and John Searle. The meaning of speech acts is derived only in the context of the speech and not in the actual words. Speech acts are performed with words such as oaths and promises. The actual words "I do" have radically different meanings when they are a response to "Do you want to eat?" versus "Do you take this man/woman . . . ?" Speech is acting, and the meaning is contingent on the context and the action. Contextualists use this analogy and argue that all text can only be understood in terms of context. They seek a broad framework for meaning, instead of a text's place within a canon of great texts. This broad framework shifts the focus from continuity to context.

Contextualists attacked the history-of-ideas tradition by emphasizing a broader history if one wishes to understand the canon of great books. Another attack involved scaling down the history of ideas beyond the great thinkers. Proponents of this method argue that second-rate thinkers are more emblematic of their cultures' basic ideas than are the so-called great figures of intellectual history.

5.2.3 New Intellectual History

The most recent challenges to the history of ideas tradition have come from (1) histories of the common person and (2) diachronic analysis of cultural elites. Histories of the ideas, attitudes, and opinions of the common person (e.g., Ginzburg, Rudé, and Lefebvre) pursue the mentality, *mentalité*, or *Zeitgeist*, which consists simply of the fundamental shared presuppositions that make up an age. These historians believe that these assumptions and attitudes existed and are now knowable even if they were rarely articulated. In *The Cheese and the Worms*, Carlo Ginzburg takes two heresy trials and the subsequent execution of a remote Friulian miller, facts that would have been at most a minor footnote in a Rankean study, recreates the miller's sixteenth-century world view, and suggests that it is representative of peasant cosmology.[26] The church itself had put the miller on trial and thereby recorded the very world view it was trying to eradicate. Ginzburg meticulously examines the semiliterate miller's ideas in the context of pre-Christian ideas and high-culture writings. The miller becomes a unique filter between high and low culture as he reads the works of high culture and filters them down to the low culture while simultaneously providing the high-culture inquisitors with a view of low-culture ideas. The work reveals the fundamental ideas of the otherwise forgotten peoples of history rather than the ideas of a few innovative thinkers. This intellectual history of the average person parallels a broader opening-up of history to include cultural factors beyond the traditional arts and literature of high culture. Intellectual history is no longer confined to analysis of the so-called great books written by a small number of great thinkers; it now includes all human thought including popular opinions and irrational ideas.

Despite the growing popularity of the history of the common person, other historians, such as Carl Schorske, have maintained a focus on elite culture. But Schorske has avoided the teleological unfolding of many intellectual historians by consistently employing the synchronic instead of the diachronic unfolding of the past even when it was not fashionable to do so. Burkhardt's synchronic was based on metaphors (politics as art, birth of the individual, illegitimacy) but Burkhardt's synchronic history maintained a diachronic unfolding within several sections (i.e., chapters on politics). In his Pulitzer-winning book *Fin-de-Siécle Vienna: Politics and Culture,* Schorske explored cultural aspects of Vienna in the late 1800s and early 1900s (the turn of the century) as individual phenomena. Critics may claim that he fails to explain causal change, but he was not interested in the diachronic origins of cultural events. He focused instead on the fact that things appear at the same time. For instance a musician's composition is not discussed in terms of how it fits into the traditional unfolding of music history and is viewed instead relative to what was happening in the world of ideas. The overall effect is that the reader comes to grasp many aspects of the intellectual and cultural milieu. The causal unfolding of intellectual traditions, neat and clear with the timelines and definitions of diverse subfields such as political history, music history, or art history, is forsaken for a somewhat messy understanding of the past. Similar to a collage or Facebook wall, this approach allows the reader to see a wide range of traits in some depth.

Schorske chooses to analyze a wide range of aspects that influence intellectual traditions rather than focusing on historical change. This allows him to define an era without precise delineation of historical change. He reveals tendencies without being trapped in diachronic periodization. This allows some readers to relish in the metaphor and others to complain that he has not showed what caused precise changes. A focus on change allows historians to evaluate winners and losers, or those who benefit from change and those who suffer due to chance, but it also forces analysis into a periodization that may work in some arenas of existence but not in others.

5.3 CULTURAL HISTORY

We have been examining two major changes in writing history: (1) the continual revision of a Rankean focus on states, politics, and elites in favor of alternative foci; and (2) the rejection of profoundly materialist social history, such as that practiced by Marxists and Annalists, who assume that culture and ideas are determined by economic and material elements in society. We have seen historians of *mentalité* who argue that an idea can be a causal force in history in its own right without recourse to materialist explanations.

The same goes for cultural historians: some argue that culture is not simply a reflection of economics, but that in fact economic and social relations are an example of cultural practices, that these various layers are, causally speaking, equally important. These cultural historians tend to follow an anthropological approach to culture that emphasizes how culture itself is part of a broader language of symbolic understanding because it is the means by which experience is organized and rendered sensible. Their point, quite simply, is that cultural historians think that culture can be studied in its own right without viewing it as a reflection of something else. The resulting studies tread a fine line between intellectual and cultural history that is united in its repudiation of Rankean history but deeply divided over the roles of material and nonmaterial causation.

5.3.1 Materialists and Nonmaterialists

Materialists examine the material realm to explain the reasons for which change occurs in other realms. A basic schema for this approach would be society as a pyramid with material forces at the foundation or base of the pyramid and social, political, and cultural factors in some hierarchical order above the economic base. Marxists see the top of the pyramid as a reflection of an economic base and thereby reject the Rankean interest in politics as a mere illusion concealing the real economic basis for change. War ceases to be a product of failed diplomacy and is instead interpreted in economic terms as a fight about profits. The Annalists undermine this emphasis on an economic base by seeking geographical factors that are yet deeper. But does such a causal pyramid in fact exist, or could the opposite be true? Could culture actually determine what happens in the economic realm?

Nonmaterialists beleive that culture is not a reflection but rather a constituent element of the past. Some of them completely reverse the pyramid by making cultural factors the determinants of economic change. Michel Foucault shows how cultural decisions can dictate economic decisions in his study of madness. Madness is a cultural decision because each culture decides who is and who is not sane. This cultural construction of "madness" becomes a determining factor in decisions such as the treatment and institutionalization of mentally ill people. Cultural decisions dictate economic decisions in this case because the definition of madness forces economic and social decisions about how people will be treated.

Carlo Ginzburg posits a different sort of causal change that maintains a strong material character without requiring that the material forces are primary. He argues that economic, social, and cultural factors change at different paces. Economic things change more quickly than social factors, while cultural elements change the slowest. The resulting lag between economic, social, and cultural elements becomes a determining factor in its own right.

The study of culture becomes more significant if social, political, and economic factors change at different paces because culture allows one to explain regional variations. For instance, if economic changes are the causal factors behind the French Revolution, then the historian is faced with explaining why the Revolution took place in France instead of the economically more developed England. Cultural historians such as Lynn Hunt reject the materialist causal pyramid and suggest that a reciprocity exists between cultural and economic factors. Culture in part determines the economy, and economic factors in part determine culture.

A Möbius strip consists of a strip of paper that has been twisted once and then taped together. If you put your finger and thumb on either side of the strip and move them around it you will find that the inside of the strip is not distinguishable from the outside. Just as the strip has no pure inside and no pure outside, so too the study of history, according to Hunt, should consist of cultural analysis that cannot be reduced to simple economic or noneconomic factors.

This fine line between materialist and nonmaterialist historians is not limited to cultural historians; other historians also emphasize the role of ideas and mentalities, but culture offers a broad and viable focal point. The advantage of no verifiable inside and outside prevents the causal oversimplifications that frequently follow material analysis. The inability to pinpoint clear causal factors, however, can result in a cultural history that is descriptive but fails to explain why things happened.

5.3.2 Subjects of Cultural History

Cultural history is much like other forms of history we have examined, but the focus is on the people instead of politics or even the social historian's focus on aspects of everyday life. The broad themes of cultural history evolved out of a nineteenth-century sensibility that local culture was being destroyed. Local, prenational cultures were threatened by the rise of railroads, mandatory education, military conscription, and rising urbanization. Local dialects, for instance, were deemed unsuitable for certain types of business and political conversations. This climate fostered a heyday of studies of local and popular culture such as Burckhardt's *The Civilization of the Renaissance in Italy*, Macaulay's *The History of England*, and the Grimm brothers' collections of local folktales and peasant stories. Folklorists like the Grimms studied local festivals, religions, and beliefs in order to preserve folk culture. "The people are poets" claimed the Grimms as they rejected analysis of intellectual elites, or high culture, in favor of the masses. They assumed that high culture was an artificial construct, whereas peasant culture was an organic entity with deep roots. The collection of tales was an attempt to understand culture much as one studies language by interpreting it and realizing that it has different meanings contingent on the country and the cultural context.

Distinctions between high and low culture have been hotly debated, but the general consensus is that they are quite fluid. For instance, is Bartok's music high or low culture? He took popular songs and turned them into "classical" music. And jazz certainly had strong origins in popular culture but currently is quite fashionable in high culture.

One solution is to study cultures, plural, with an awareness of separate cultures, or subcultures, within cultures. Anthropologist Robert Redfield distinguishes between (1) great culture (elite culture) and (2) little culture that consists of all other cultures. But the lines between the two are not that clear. Mikhail Bakhtin studied the reciprocity between a high and low culture in his book *Rabelais and His World* by analyzing peasant chapbooks and Rabelais's books *Gargantua* (1533) and *Pantagruel* (1535).[27] Bakhtin revealed a multiplicity of voices and showed the existence of reciprocity between the official discourse of high culture (king, church, and intellectuals) and the profane language of popular culture (carnivals and popular festivals). Menochio, the Friulian miller whom Ginzburg studied in *The Cheese and the Worms*, clearly floated between high and low cultures acting as a filter through which high and low cultures interacted. Such filters are necessary for solid historical analysis because traditional popular culture was an oral culture that left few fragments for contemporary analysis.

Stephen Kern's *The Culture of Time and Space, 1880–1918* offers an intriguing analysis of high culture that has implications for low culture.[28] Kern outlines a shift in two basic ideas of our culture: time and space. Time poses a paradox because of the development of two types of time: (1) standard time with its hourly gradations, which is actually local time; and (2) modern time, which is private and idiosyncratic. Kern analyzes novels and scientific ideas of high culture to show that modern private time is not standardized with other times. Oscar Wilde's *The Picture of*

Dorian Gray has two sets of time: (1) portrait time, which is private; and (2) Gray's time, which is public. Marcel Proust's *Remembrance of Things Past* contains a dualistic framework mixing standard time with recollections of childhood. Proust himself worked in a corked room and rarely ventured out, but he had an uncanny memory of childhood events. James Joyce's *Ulysses* places the experiences of Ulysses's lifetime into one day of Stephen's life. Psychoanalysis brings the past into the present by suggesting that the past is a real part of our subconscious present. And Einstein's relativity makes time contingent on the speed of acceleration of the body.

Kern offers an equally convincing argument about space: the modern notion of an atom is something with space in it; hence, atoms are not building blocks—they are more space than solid. Architects now think of space as something they can sculpt and create. Space changes from the absence of buildings to a positive entity that can be used creatively. Frederick Jackson Turner's thesis about the American frontier contends that the Western frontier was crucial to American mentality because it was a *safety valve*, a vast space for expansion. Changes in the perception of time and space, then, are obvious both in science and in artistic expressions such as literature, painting, and music. Kern assumes that culture is a unitary whole and that we are living in the past—that all various cultural endeavors reflect some common cultural mind-set. But do novelists, scientists, and architects reflect the same cultural reality as each other, much less all other people?

5.4 PSYCHOHISTORY AND ITS DISCONTENTS

Psychohistory is basically the application of Freudian analysis to historical individuals or groups of people in pursuit of nonmaterialist factors beyond the state and politics. The close association with psychoanalysis means that psychohistory is subject to the same animosity and attacks that psychoanalysis faces. Moreover, while Freudian psychohistory predominates, psychohistory need not be Freudian; hence, it is open to criticism from followers of Adler, Jung, Lacan, and other fashionable theorists.

Another major hurdle that psychohistorians face centers on whether their analysis of history is really historical. Freud emphasized an *unconscious mind* consisting of unconscious human motivations. His conscious–unconscious dualism actually consisted of three components: (1) *id*, the unconscious self;, (2) *ego*, the conscious self; and (3) *superego*, the outward projection of the self. The role of the id is central because it is the basis of our psychic life. Our childhood experience and development form a subconscious self that is often in conflict with the ego and superego. For instance, repression is simply the ego and super-ego telling us not to think or act in a certain manner. A Freudian slip or a dream involves censored material, frequently consisting of infan-tile sexual desire, emerging in disguised form. Other outbursts of cen-sored material may produce neurotic behavior or even creative activity. Freud's famous Oedipus and Electra complexes are the unconscious and repressed desire to kill the same-sex parent and gain the sole affection of the opposite-sex parent. A psychohistorian who examines the past with Freudian assumptions may jump to conclusions about motives that are supported by Freudian theory but not by other evidence. Moreover, historians frequently dismiss Freud's assumptions about human nature as misleading, and feminists find his patriarchal and misogynist beliefs irrelevant to studies of anything other than Freud's own culture.

Freud himself wrote a classic example of psychohistory when he reconstructed Leonardo da Vinci's youth in a 1910 study.[29] Little is known of the young Leonardo, so much of the work consists of conjec-ture and leaps of faith, but Freud did offer new types of evidence and a new way of thinking about Leonardo. We do know that he was an ille-gitimate child born in 1452. According to Freud, da Vinci questioned his origins and who his real father was. This fact combined with latent homosexuality meant he had no real sex life but a profound pursuit of knowledge, painting, and science. These drives contributed to making him into an imaginative scientist and researcher. The greatest problem of this amazingly tight line of thinking is that certain words were grossly mistranslated into Freud's native German, such as turning a nonvulture into a vulture. Freud makes much of a vulture that is the product of bad linguistics. Changing the word should require destruction of the theory and the creation of the new theory. Psychohistorians create tidy explana-tions of the past, but are they correct?

David Stannard's *Shrinking History* is an attack on psychohistory that includes a critique of Freud's study of Leonardo.[30] Stannard shows that all we can know from the sources Freud used is that Leonardo was curious and spent some of his money on students. Leonardo left no records of sexual history and cannot be analyzed. Unfortunately, Stannard's interpretation is less than inspiring, and he fails to contribute any sense of the imagination and creative use of limited evidence that exists in Freud's study.

Henry Preserved Smith wrote a psychohistory of Luther in 1913, shortly after Freud's analysis of Leonardo, but the psychohistory move-ment gathered steam in 1930 due to the appearance of Erik Erikson's popular book *Young Man Luther* and a speech by William Langer at the American Historical Association.[31] Langer's address to professional historians argued that history should take the unconscious as one of its tools. This speech, along with the controversial success of Erikson's book, turned psychohistory into the black sheep of reactions to Rankean history. Relatively few historians are trained psychoanalysts and thus psychohistorians are rarely held in high esteem by practicing psychoanalysts. Peter Lowenberg, a psychoanalyst with a Ph.D. in history, has been one of the few to maintain recognition in both fields. Psychohistory has not lived up to the early expectations as skeptical historians have failed to believe Freud's assumptions and theories.

Jeffrey Masson, a Berkeley psychoanalyst and former director of the Freud archive, used letters and other documents to attack Freud's assumptions about infant psychology.[32] Freud claimed that infants have fantasy sex lives: children have strong sexual interests and feelings. He based these claims on female patients' recollections of infant seduction scenes. The problem is that these memories may not have been fantasy. Freud was reluctant to face the possibility that his patients had actually been sexually abused as children. Freud failed to deal with the possibility of child abuse, opting instead to develop a theory of childhood fantasies that might not help patients who had actually been abused.

Feminists have further problems with psychoanalysis because Freud's theory is sexist: women are viewed as incomplete men because they lack a penis, motherhood is the destiny of women, and women's moral authority is less than that of men. Freud's theories are also extremely patriarchal. Belief in Freudian psychohistory requires faith in Freud's sexist assumptions and theories.

On the other hand, many of Freud's concepts have become part of our language and culture. Richard Cobb loathes psychohistory and Freudian methodology, yet he uses Freudian terms such as "death wish." G. R. Elton is not a Freudian, yet he speaks of *unconscious* attitudes. Many historians who reject psychohistory still use Freudian language because terms like "Freudian slip," "Oedipus complex," "ego," "superego," and "id" have become a staple part of the English language. In *Thomas Jefferson: An Intimate History*, Fawn Brodie looks at Thomas Jefferson's journals and notes that Jefferson used the word *mulatto* when describing a journey in France.[33] Jefferson had an affair with his mulatto slave Sally, and she was not with him in France. The journals could therefore reveal how much this woman was on his mind. Garry Wills rejects this interpretation and explains that "mulatto" was a common term for the description of landscapes at that time and Jefferson was in an area of France known for its "mulatto" landscapes; hence, there is no need to invoke psychohistory. We have a great deal of evidence about Jefferson, but the use of psychohistory here does provide an imaginative twist and one that can certainly be fruitful in situations with more limited evidence.

One problem with attempting to psychoanalyze individuals from the past is the fact that psychoanalysis involves a dialogue between the doctor and patient. This dialogue requires a living, thinking person.

The meagerness of details left by most individuals makes any attempt to reconstruct a plausible dialogue futile. But what about psychohistory that goes beyond biography and examines collective phenomena? Theodor Adorno looked at the authoritarian personality in his theory of why certain countries bred stronger leaders than others.[34] German fascist leaders in this analysis are emblematic of the society that they led. Rudolph Binion's *Hitler among the Germans* is a psychobiography of the followers of Hitler.[35] Perhaps the most successful example of collective analysis is Robert Wohl's psychoanalytic sociology in *The Generation of 1914*.[36] Wohl looks at the whole generation as a cohort and delineates plausible psychological explanations.

But can historians really put individuals, much less whole generations, on the analyst's couch? Certainly historians cannot analyze the dead in the same way psychoanalysts question their patients, but they can apply psychoanalytic assumptions and terminology to the past. These assumptions pose a daunting problem because the entire audience must accept the same assumptions about human nature for the conclusions to be valid. Freud assumes that human nature does not change. His term "Oedipus complex" defines a universal trait that is characteristic of small boys who want to kill their fathers and sleep with their mothers. This is based on assumptions of rivalry between son and father, but do other family structures possess this same idea?

Ernest Jones, a staunch Freudian, defended this definition of the Oedipal complex in a debate with Bronislaw Malinowski, a famous anthropologist. Malinowski argued that the Oedipal complex is a product of the society and defended this view with research into the Trobriand Islands. On the Trobriand Islands, the conflict was between mother, son, and mother's brother, not between father and son. In fact, fathers and sons shared interests and thus were allies instead of enemies. Historians have challenged assumptions about human nature by tracing evolving notions of guilt and shame (Norbert Elias), changing conceptions of love and affection (Lawrence Stone), and various notions of childhood (Philippe Ariès). The failure to maintain a dialogue with the past, like the dialogue between patient and psychoanalyst, forces psychohistorians to rely on controversial assumptions about human nature and the universality of certain traits.

Assumptions about universality pose a further problem for psychohistorians because such assumptions frequently lead to anachronistic history. John Demos, a historian of witchcraft, assumes in his study of Salem, New England, that people today share the same sense of "turf" or "living space" as people of that time.[37] He therefore concludes that the crowded conditions in Salem made people nasty, especially within their own family. This theory is intriguing, but it is also nonfalsifiable: you can neither refute it nor prove it once you accept the assumption.

Karl Popper analyzes the problem of falsifiability when creating theories. He argues that you need positive evidence but you also need to give examples under which the theory would still be correct if something different had happened. Positive evidence might be that because the sun comes up in the morning it rotates around the earth. Posing potential conditions that would disprove this belief are necessary to make a theory testable. The absence of potential negative ideas is what distinguishes, say, astronomy from astrology: one can be wrong and one cannot. Some critics of psychoanalysis claim that psychoanalysis is not really science because it cannot be proven wrong.

Psychohistory faces tough problems from an audience of historians because of problems of falsifiability, the ahistorical characteristic of its assumptions about human nature and universality, and the inability to put dead individuals or groups on a couch for interactive analysis. Perhaps the greatest problem is the grandiose claims that psychohistorians have made about its potential application. Nevertheless, psychohistory does have a great deal to offer: adding psychological explanations to a cadre of other potential factors provides refreshing new perspectives, and the ability to theorize about generational traits and mind-sets has certainly contributed to our understanding of history.

5.5 COMPARATIVE HISTORY

Comparative history offers historians one of the better responses to universalizing theories because it balances analysis of broad traits and trends while still maintaining the ability to highlight historical specificity. Comparisons allow historians to reconcile the tension between sociology and history. They become the historians' answer to historical sociology. The central point for effective comparisons is to isolate crucial factors from merely incidental ones. For this purpose, comparison functions for historians much as experimentation does for the scientist. By delineating similarities and differences the historian is able to pinpoint causal factors that might not be evident in the myopia of individual studies.

The logic of this delineation of causal factors, and the logic of comparative history in general, is consistent with the methods of agreement and difference that J. S. Mill described in his *Philosophy of Scientific Method*. Mill defined a method of agreement: if two instances of an event have only one factor in common, then this is the crucial factor. This is the opposite of his method of difference: if there are two instances in which an event occurs and then does not occur and they are alike in all respects but one, then that respect is the cause of the event. Comparison thus becomes a tool for delineating the causal factors that were so elusive to nonmaterialist, cultural historians.

Marc Bloch extended Mill's comparative method to fit actual historical issues. He distinguished two kinds of comparison: (1) between remote societies and (2) between closely related societies. Closely related societies can be approached by concrete comparisons such as the patterns of land enclosure in rural England and France. Comparisons between remote societies are a quest for similarities that cannot be explained by a common origin or mutual influence. Historians then seek similar situations in remote societies to consider common motives that are frequently of a material instead of ideological nature. For instance, Ginzburg's analysis of the Friulian miller suggests that a peasant materialist view of the world existed in Friuli (a region in northeastern Italy) that was shared with other peasant societies. These views were considered heretical yet they were widespread across Europe; hence, the peasant materialist view of the world can be attributed neither to Christianity nor to specific local factors. Comparisons of this type allow historians to consider the general causes of general phenomena or, in other words, to see the forest without being blinded by the particulars of the trees.

But wait, you say; history only deals with the unique. The comparative historian is sure to respond that the very concept of "unique" rests on implicit comparison. A third method of comparative history involves implicit comparisons within one society that are as comparative as any juxtapositions between different societies. Werner Sombart's 1906 *Why Is There No Socialism in the United States?*[38] and Max Weber's article "The Protestant Sects and the Spirit of Capitalism" (not to be confused with his more famous book *The Protestant Ethic and the Spirit of Capitalism*) are actually implicit comparisons between Germany and the United States.[39] A more recent comparison between the two is Jürgen Kocka's *White Collar Workers in America, 1890–1940*, purportedly a study of workers in the United States that actually shows the position of German white-collar workers in the 1930s.[40]

Comparative history requires choosing meaningful comparisons that add to our understanding of the past. A less effective method of comparative history consists of comparisons that are used to throw additional facts at you instead of adding to an argument. Such works frequently attack accepted theories but do so in a fashion that does not provide a more meaningful perspective; they simply force historians to consider additional facts to maintain a thesis. For instance, Arno Mayer's *The Persistence of the Old Regime* attacks the standard thesis that more and more people were brought into political participation in Europe, thereby creating (1) increased democratization and (2) increased exclusion of the aristocrats.[41] Mayer's comparative solution is that the evolution of European politics has not been progressing toward better government. He rejects the standard position but fails to direct historians to do more than seek additional facts.

Comparative history at its best offers the scope and emphasis of sociology and the distinctiveness of history. Peter Kolchin's *Unfree Labor* is a brilliantly executed history of American slavery and Russian serfdom.[42] Kolchin presents serfdom and slavery as products of increased demand from European markets. The ensuing increased demand for laborers resulted in two different methods of controlling labor. The economic reasons for slavery in North America were related to the European labor market as European indentured servants were brought over and had to work off the cost of their journey. Both American slavery and Russian serfdom were products of the need for labor, but the differences are significant: (1) racial distinctions were used in America, (2) serfs were a local majority while slaves were a minority from outside the region, (3) serfs had more rights and a less formal system of control, and (4) serf estates were much larger than plantations and were more frequently owned by absentee landowners. Kolchin successfully provides two separate stories of great interest and shows an interaction between them that creates more than just the sum of their parts.

Another example of comparative history that maintains historical specificity as well as implications for contemporary society is Norbert Elias's two-volume *The Civilizing Process*.[43] Elias traces the evolution of polite behavior in European society with a focus on the extent to which natural instincts have been tamed and brought under control. The evolution of a lower threshold of shame is evident in the development of table manners and personal hygiene. The sorts of control of basic bodily functions that Europeans absorb in childhood were not always practiced and, according to Elias, first began to be inculcated during the early modern period. The overall point is to recognize the degree to which our sense of freedom, meaning the absence of external restraints on our behavior, was made possible only by the suppression of instincts and desires that, if acted upon, would make unconstrained and unpoliced social intercourse impossible. The "civilizing process" consists of internal repression relative to previous generations who were more afraid of outside threats than internal threats. Thomas Haskell follows Elias's lead and extends the notion of civilizing process beyond manners into slavery, and John Kasson's *Rudeness and Civility* brings Elias's methods and basic premise to an analysis of the United States.[44]

The combination of comparative scope, contemporary significance, and impetus for further research is also found in Robert I. Moore's *The Formation of a Persecuting Society*.[45] Moore presents the rise of intolerant Western societies that accept the persecution and exclusion of unwanted minorities. The origins, according to Moore, are to be found in a three-hundred-year period beginning in the thirteenth century when Christians began persecuting heretics as well as Jews, lepers, and homosexuals. Critics contend that this is a form of reverse Whiggism and that

Moore has constructed too narrow a framework. The current consensus is that persecution came in waves and that a wider framework would have revealed equally valid examples of persecution prior to the purported formation of a persecuting society. The thesis remains intriguing despite these drawbacks because it offers a plausible explanation for heightened persecution. Furthermore, it challenges readers to consider persecution and potential persecution in their contemporary society.

The new varieties of history have forced all historians to recognize that the past may be viewed from a wide range of possible explanations. The best exemplars of each variety frequently push the method to levels that are unacceptable to some historians. This expansion of the boundaries of history prevents historians from becoming too complacent in their analysis of the past. History that combines comparative scope, methodological rigor, historicist pursuit of the past's otherness, and awareness of implications for the present should serve as a model for widening the context of discussion beyond specific fields of study.

NOTES

1. Fernand Braudel, "Histoire et sciences sociales—La longue durée," *Annales: Economies, Sociéties, Civilisations* 13 (1958): 725–753.

2. François Furet, "Beyond the Annales," *Journal of Modern History* 55 (September 1983): 391.

3. Le Roy Ladurie is relatively close to the positivists in that he does not argue that history's relation to the present is one of the ingredients of its relation to truth.

4. Emmanuel Le Roy Ladurie, *The Peasants of Languedoc*, trans. with an introduction by John Day (Urbana, IL: University of Illinois Press, 1974).

5. Marc Leopold Benjamin Bloch, *Feudal Society*, trans. L. A. Manyon, foreword by M. M. Postan (Chicago: University of Chicago Press, 1961); and Lucien Paul Victor Febvre,*The Problem of Unbelief in the Sixteenth Century, the Religion of Rabelais*, trans. Beatrice Gottlieb (Cambridge, MA: Harvard University Press, 1982).

6. Fernand Braudel, *The Mediterranean and the Mediterranean World in the Age of Philip II* (New York: Harper & Row, 1972).

7. Emmanuel Le Roy Ladurie, *Histoire du climat depuis l'an mil* (Paris: Flammarion, 1967).

8. David W. Sabean, *Power in the Blood: Popular Culture and Village Discourse in Early Modern Germany* (Cambridge: Cambridge University Press, 1984).

9. Baron Thomas Babington Macaulay is best known for his Whig-utilitarian historical thesis: the substance of history is material progress, and that progress is attainable via the application of particular political principles. *The History of England* (New York: Penguin Books, 1968).

10. E. P. Thompson, *The Making of the English Working Class* (New York: Random House, 1963).

11. Georges Lefebvre, *The Great Fear of 1789: Rural Panic in Revolutionary France* (Princeton, NJ: Princeton University Press, 1973).

12.   George Rudé, *The Crowd in the French Revolution* (Oxford: Clarendon Press, 1959). See also Rudé's *Paris and London in the Eighteenth Century: Studies in Popular Protest* (New York: Viking Press, 1971).
13.   William Sheridan Allen, *The Nazi Seizure of Power: The Experience of a Single German Town, 1922–1945*, rev. edn. (New York: F. Watts, 1984).
14.   Daniel Goldhagen, *Hitler's Willing Executioners: Ordinary Germans and the Holocaust* (New York: Random House, 1996).
15.   Detlev Peukert, "Youth in the Third Reich," in Richard Bessel's *Life in the Third Reich* (Oxford: Oxford University Press, 1987), pp. 25–40.
16.   Johan Galtung and Sohail Inayatullah, *Macrohistory and Macrohistorians: Perspectives on Individual, Social, and Civilizational Change* (Westport, Connecticut: Praeger, 1997), p. 159.
17.   Ibid., p. 1.
18.   David Christian, "The Case for 'Big History,'" *Journal of World History* 2 (1991): 223–238.
19.   Randall Collins, *Macrohistory: Essays in Sociology of the Long Run* (Stanford: Stanford University Press, 1999), p. 7.
20.   One of the best recent reviews of macrohistory is Gale Stokes, "The Fates of Human Societies: A Review of Recent Macrohistories,"*American Historical Review* 106 (2001): 508–526.
21.   Peter Burke, *History and Social Theory* (Ithaca, NY: Cornell University Press, 1992), p. 38.
22.   On the early development of microhistory, see Carlo Ginzburg, "Microhistory: Two or Three Things That I Know about It," *Critical Inquiry* 20 (1993): 10–35. For a student-friendly overview of Ginzburg's theory of history, see Carlo Ginzburg, *History, Rhetoric, and Proof: The Menahem Stern Jerusalem Lectures* (Hanover, NH: University Press of New England, 1999). For a delightful, albeit polemical, call for French historians to consider the microhistorical methodology of the Italians, see Carlo Ginzburg and Marco Ferrari's "The Dovecote Has Opened Its Eyes," in Edward Muir and Guido Ruggiero's *Microhistory and the Lost Peoples of Europe* (Baltimore: Johns Hopkins University Press, 1991).
23.   For Ginzburg's description of his own methodology see Carlo Ginzburg's *Clues, Myths, and the Historical Method*, trans. John and Anne C. Tedeschi (Baltimore: Johns Hopkins University Press, 1989), here p. 105.
24.   Arthur O. Lovejoy, *The Great Chain of Being: A Study of the History of an Idea* (Cambridge, MA: Harvard University Press, 1936).
25.   Quentin Skinner, *The Foundations of Modern Political Thought* (Cambridge: Cambridge University Press, 1978).
26.   Carlo Ginzburg, *The Cheese and the Worms: The Cosmos of a Sixteenth-Century Miller* (New York: Penguin Books, 1982 [c. 1980]).
27.   Mikhail Bakhtin, *Rabelais and His World*, trans. Hélène Iswolsky (Cambridge, MA: MIT Press, 1968).
28.   Stephen Kern, *The Culture of Time and Space, 1880–1918: With a New Preface* (Cambridge, MA: Harvard University Press, 1983).
29.   Sigmund Freud, *Leonardo da Vinci and a Memory of His Childhood* (New York: Norton, 2003).
30.   David E. Stannard, *Shrinking History: On Freud and the Failure of Psychohistory* (New York: Oxford University Press, 1980).

31.   Henry Preserved Smith, *Luther's Early Development in the Light of Psycho-Analysis* (Champaign, IL: University of Illinois Press, 1913[?]), reprinted in *American Journal of Psychology* 24 (1913); and Erik H. Erikson, *Young Man Luther: A Study in Psychoanalysis and History* (New York: W. W. Norton & Co., 1958).

32.   J. Moussaieff Masson, *The Assault on Truth: Freud's Suppression of the Seduction Theory* (New York: Penguin Books, 1985).

33.   Fawn McKay Brodie, *Thomas Jefferson: An Intimate History* (New York: W. W. Norton & Co., 1974).

34.   Theodor Adorno, *The Authoritarian Personality* (New York: Harper & Bros., 1952).

35.   Rudolph Binion, *Hitler among the Germans* (New York: Elsevier, 1976).

36.   Robert Wohl, *The Generation of 1914* (Cambridge, MA: Harvard University Press, 1979).

37.   John Demos, *Entertaining Satan: Witchcraft and the Culture of Early New England* (New York: Oxford University Press, 1982).

38.   Werner Sombart, *Why Is There No Socialism in the United States?*, trans. Patricia M. Hocking and C. T. Husbands (White Plains, NY: International Arts and Sciences Press, 1976).

39.   Max Weber's article and book are published together in one volume translated by Stephen Kalberg, *The Protestant Ethic and the Spirit of Capitalism*, 3rd edn. (Los Angeles: Roxbury, 2002).

40.   Jürgen Kocka, *White Collar Workers in America, 1890–1940: A Social-Political History in International Perspective*, trans. Maura Kealey (London: Sage Publications, 1980).

41.   Arno J. Mayer, *The Persistence of the Old Regime: Europe to the Great War* (New York: Pantheon Books, 1981).

42.   Peter Kolchin, *Unfree Labor: American Slavery and Russian Serfdom* (Cambridge, MA: Belknap Press of Harvard University Press, 1987).

43.   Norbert Elias, *The Civilizing Process*, trans. Edmund Jephcott (Oxford: B. Blackwell, 1994).

44.   John F. Kasson, *Rudeness and Civility: Manners in Nineteenth-Century Urban America* (New York: Hill and Wang, 1990).

45.   Robert I. Moore, *The Formation of a Persecuting Society: Power and Deviance in Western Europe, 950–1250* (Cambridge, MA: Basil Blackwell, 1987).

Chapter 6

Historical Actors

Having heard your acquaintances' various histories of what happened to your roommate, you return later to the same restaurant for a cup of coffee and a chance to contemplate alone your roommate's departure. The different accounts shed some light on the roommate conundrum, and you are thankful for the various historical contexts provided, but you still lack a definitive explanation of what caused the specific actions at exactly that time. You lack a precise focus on the agents of change, and now that your roommate is gone, you are uncertain about your own understanding of your roommate's motivations. Certainly your roommate was rational, or are you deluded into seeking a rational explanation for an irrational person? Does your roommate really think like you do, or are your thoughts a product of your economic class or social status? What do you actually know about your roommate's economic resources and family connections? How can one really know another's true allegiances, much less one's sexual proclivities? What is the difference between sex and gender? Was your roommate driven by sexual desire or by a social construction of appropriate gender? Why merely gender? What about the entire nexus of social constructions that was spun around your roommate?

This all leads to the question of historical actor. Should you attempt to define your roommate's action because of the fact that the two of you shared an apartment, or should you define your roommate by rationality, class, gender, or some other factor? In other words, how would your roommate rationalize action, and how would you rationalize action? Is it possible that conscious rationalizations are not consistent with true motivations, that your ex-post-facto rationalizations (formulated after the actions) for why you ordered the dessert you now eat with your coffee are not consistent with the real impulse that created the original decision to order the dessert?

The discrepancy between motivations and ex-post-facto rationalizations poses serious problems when historians attempt to explain why things happened. The very act of choosing specific historical actors produces a biased perspective on the causes of potential changes in the past. Upon which historical actors should historians focus and why? Is there anything that cannot be the object of historical analysis? We turn next to four ways of viewing actors in history: (1) rationality, (2) class, (3) gender, and (4) structures of perception.

6.1 RATIONAL ACTORS

The law of parsimony, or Occam's razor as it has come to be called, is the simple principle that there is no need to make an argument more complicated than is necessary to make your point. When faced with two competing theories, a person should prefer the simplest one, and when attempting to explain the unknown, a person should begin with what is already known. People are rational, for if they were irrational, why pursue a field of study that attempts to rationalize what is known to be irrational? Rational-choice theory is taken from a branch of economics and political science that explains rational behavior in the economic and political realms. Some historians take the assumptions of rational-choice theory and apply them to the past. Before doing so, it is worth analyzing the assumptions behind rational-choice theory: (1) people are rational, (2) people act individually, (3) all collectives ultimately can be studied in terms of the individuals that make up the collective, and (4) individuals are utility maximizers.

The implications of these four points allow scholars to study individual behavior in the voting booth or at the bank and then make predictions about what individuals will do in the future. People are rational and are therefore able to order their preferences to achieve as many of their high priorities as possible because they will behave in a rational manner. If people ultimately take action based on individual rationality, then all collectives can be viewed in terms of the individuals that make up the collective, assuming those individuals (a) have the possibility of choice and (b) are not restricted by structural restraints and determinations. Last, human beings are utility maximizers who seek maximum profits or maximum personal interests. The four main assumptions appear logical, but the scope of their application in history is worthy of further consideration.

Mancur Olson revises this common-sense theory slightly by applying rational-choice theory to collectives. In *The Logic of Collective Action* he rejects the assumption that groups are motivated by the same interest and logic as individuals.[1] Group self-interest and specifically groups trying to maximize self-interests are problematic because of the existence of "free riders." In fact, all public goods are bedeviled by free riders who individually do not join a group if they can share the benefit of the group without incurring the cost of membership. If there is no reason to join based on individual rational interest, then free riders will not join. This kind of thinking poses a daunting problem for public goods like clean air, police, defense, or mass transit. Why join if you can reap the benefits without paying the price?

The collective-action dilemma is based on the belief that rational workers will not act in a group. There is a difference between individual and group rationality because, although it is rational for the group to have all workers join, the individual worker gets the highest return by not joining others in a union. Olson argues that while common interests may appear, classes will never appear: shared common interests do not imply that it is rational to join together and act. Based on game theory, it appears that the size of a group is the key to cooperation: the larger the group, the harder it is to know the interests of all involved; hence, it is more difficult to know if your defection from the group will be retaliated against. It is individually rational to cooperate in a large group only if you know that your defection will cause others to defect and in so doing possibly jeopardize your access to the public good provided by the group.

Olson presents various "rational" theories of groups that explain that cooperation can be rational and can emerge over time. The *causal variant* claims that there is an *instinct* or *tendency* to join groups. The *formal variant* claims that there was development from small kinship groups to larger societal groups. This position, constantly reformulated by functionalists, posits that groups serve various functions. A third variant is the *traditional*, which claims that participation in voluntary associations is universal and that while groups differ in degree, they do not differ in kind. Based on a discussion of the efficiency of providing collective goods, game theory suggests that the size of the group is key. A collective good will be provided if the gain to the group is greater than the total cost by more than it exceeds gains to any individual. Because the gain to an individual exceeds the total cost of providing the collective good to the group, groups are not efficient. The larger the group, the smaller the ability of that group to provide an optimal amount of a collective good. Because of a larger group's decreasing ability to provide the optimal supply of a collective good, it must rely on coercion or outside incentives.

This theory of individual versus collective rationality has profound implications for Marxist social theory. Rationality theory rejects the idea that rational members will achieve concerted revolutionary action because to do so would be irrational individually. It is not rational for all members to rebel, even if every member of the proletariat realizes that revolution is in the best interest of the proletariat, so the rational act is to let the others incur the risks of rebellion. Olson claims that "when the class-oriented action Marx predicted does not materialize, it does *not* indicate that the economic motivation is not predominant, as some of his critics imply, but rather that there are *no* individual economic *incentives* for class action."[2] From this perspective, Marx was wrong unless his theory was really one of irrational and uneconomic class action.

The problem of free riders or those who will reap benefits without incurring the costs is explained in Garret Hardin's short article on population growth "The Tragedy of the Commons."[3] The title obviously refers to the historical demise of the common fields in the English countryside, and the article suggests a parallel between those fields and the earth today.

The commons were communally owned pastures used for grazing. Each herdsman would naturally "try to keep as many cattle as possible on the commons." The tragedy of the commons arises when social stability "becomes a reality" and checks on population growth, such as disease and tribal war, are overcome. At that point, the logic of the commons generates tragedy because each herdsman, seeking to maximize individual gain, "concludes that the only sensible course for him to pursue is to add another animal to his herd." For each herdsman, the positive benefit of doing so is one more animal, whereas the negative component, in terms of wear and tear to the pasture, is only a fraction of the individual cost because the field was communally owned. "Therein is the tragedy. Each man is locked into a system that compels him to increase his herd without limit—in a world that is limited."

Hardin concludes that freedom in a commons brings ruin to all associated with a commons. He then extrapolates to the problem of population growth on a planet with limited resources. Individuals who maximize will make efforts to be a free rider. Just as individuals overgrazed the commons, so too will they have more children than is in the best interest of society. Hardin concludes that the world's population problem cannot be solved in a technical way: optimum population is less than maximum population, so government needs to interfere with individual choice in the realm of population growth.

The implications of the free rider for historical analysis are significant in subjects like revolutions and collective behavior. Are revolutions examples of the masses rising up as one, or are they, in fact, the actions of small bands of dedicated conspirators who need to force a revolution because the free-rider tendency prevents others from risking their lives? This question also necessitates new explanations for successful collective action such as trade unions. In Germany, these cradle-to-grave social organizations are powerful not merely because they further workers' interests but also because workers join to be part of a group. The workers may be interested in individual maximizing but they join organizations because they are also interested in being part of a group.

Revolutions and trade unions share a political dimension, and it is in the realm of political decision making that rational-choice theory provides the most fruitful contribution. For instance, the *voter's paradox* seeks to explain how combinations in a coalition government will vote if the parties have different priorities. Say the three parties differ on the hierarchical importance of welfare, defense, and culture. Compromise would appear to be the solution to logical problems about support for the three issues, but traditional compromise does not seem to work when decisions are made on a simple majority basis. A coalition between two of the three parties ensures that two of the three priorities are funded while the third one is excluded. For instance, welfare and defense may be funded while culture is not. Logrolling, not compromise, predominates, and deals are cut whereby some are rewarded for giving up certain preferences and in return they are granted support for their preferences. Instead of true compromise, the parties return to "saddle points," positions from which neither group can move without losing points. Instead of finding common ground, the parties sit at their saddle points and veer as little as possible until one party is rolled off the log. The result is that two of the three may succeed with the third party receiving nothing.

Logrolling means that decisions are made by rolling a party off the log instead of seeking compromise between parties and funding portions of all three agendas. The result is that parties do not pursue traditional compromise and opt instead to hunker down at their saddle points to avoid being rolled off the log. A concrete example is the way that highway bills traditionally pass through the Congress in the United States. Individual politicians refuse to accept the bill unless something is beneficial for their district. This is a classic example of logrolling where votes are traded to achieve passage of a bill containing individual projects that reward supporters while punishing any dissent by withholding projects in opponents' districts. The result is collective action that may be contrary to the actual wishes of all individuals involved.

Rational people acting as individuals may maximize utility in a fashion that explains collective behavior in some realms of analysis, but what about instances where allegiances are based on belief instead of economic calculation? Rational-choice theory, collective rationality, the voter's paradox, and the role of free riders offer some intriguing perspectives on political and economic questions, but they also assume that politics will function correctly. Are all politicians "normal," and does this theory apply to all politics? Can it apply to, say, Hitler?

6.2 CLASS

Karl Marx's ideas, traced in Chapter 3, have had a profound influence on the writing of history. His influence peaked in the 1960s and 1970s when a social-scientific approach to history dominated the profession and a platform for change was prevalent among younger scholars. Marx is known for a saying about Ludwig Feuerbach's influence on his thought: "Philosophers have only interpreted the world in various ways, the point is to change it." One of the reasons that his ideas have been successful in creating change is that they have evolved greatly over time. A popular variation of Marx's adage is descriptive of what has actually happened: "philosophers have only interpreted Marx's ideas in various ways, the point is to change them."

The simple manipulation of Marx's definition of class has produced a range of "Marxists" who emphasize different factors responsible for the appearance of class action. Marx claimed that *economic conditions* have *transformed* the mass of people into a group sharing a *common situation* and *common interests*. The working class is a mere mass until it acquires consciousness and becomes a class-for-itself:

> This mass is thus already a class as against capital, but not for itself. In the struggle . . . this mass becomes united, and constitutes itself as a class for itself. The interests it defends become class interests. But the struggle of class against class is a political struggle.[4]

The distinction between class-in-itself and class-for-itself that Marx outlined in *The Poverty of Philosophy* has traditionally been interpreted in terms of an objective and economic *base* that is transformed into a class characterized by organization and consciousness of solidarity. The Second International codified a deterministic description of class relations, or positions in the relations of production that define interests, whereby class-in-itself transformed spontaneously and inevitably into class-for-itself. V. I. Lenin argued just the opposite of the Second International, claiming that this progression is neither spontaneous nor inevitable; hence, it is the party's role to organize. Other theorists conceived of the issue in terms of a shift from objective, economic determination into subjective class relations that are both political and ideological. Karl Kautsky claimed that capitalism divides societies into economic groups, which are then organized into classes. The dilemma for historians is in part how to identify the categories whose interests are most susceptible to class organization, be they economic, ideological, or political.

Historians such as Maurice Dobb, R. H. Hilton, Christopher Hill, and E. P. Thompson analyze class as something that is fluid, not static, and evolving over time. They therefore attack Marx's deterministic linkage of the base causing change to percolate upward to the super-structure. Classes that are independent and autonomous need not be reduced to economic determinism. For instance, E. P. Thompson attempted to save class as an ideal but attacked it as a sociological idea. His *The Making of the English Working Class* suggested that class is not a static given throughout history; it is something that is created.[5] He rejected pure class in terms of economic underpinnings because members of a class can come from different backgrounds, if they share the fact that they are in the process of becoming a class. There is no clear class consciousness that results from economic position because class is based on shared experiences instead of economic determinism. A reciprocal relationship exists between the circumstances that members of a social group experience and their consciousness of that situation. Class consciousness is thus formed by an interaction of culture and economics, which means an interaction of base and superstructure. Classes make themselves, yet they do not create themselves out of nothing. Thompson dramatically revised Marx's notion of class determined by economic position and suggested that class can have its own consciousness.

E. P. Thompson thus shifted the economic determinism to a question of moral economy as he forged a position, between Lenin and the Second International, whereby the transition to class-for-itself progresses spontaneously but not inevitably. Class can be understood only as "a social and cultural formation, arising from processes which can only be studied as they work themselves out over a considerable historical period."[6] Thompson is concerned only with class-for-itself and not with class-in-itself "because class is a cultural as much as an economic formation."[7] Only when a group develops a consciousness of common conditions and interests is it to be considered a class. Thompson considers individuals to be members of a class when they form "an active historical subject," while structuralist-Marxists, such as J. A. Cohen, consider them structurally to be a class even if they are not conscious of it.

Marx believed that class conflict leading to revolution is spontaneous and inevitable. It happens suddenly, and it must happen. Lenin, in contrast, rejected both the spontaneity and the inevitability and thus called on a vanguard of professional revolutionaries to foster the revolution. Thompson believed that, although the revolution is not inevitable, it is spontaneous. He turned the focus to a moral economy whereby norms and values, instead of pure economics, create class. Spontaneity means that those who share experiences will join the revolution, but the lack of inevitability means that humans need to be motivated to take action. Humans thus make their own history, and historians can influence this process by writing history in a manner that motivates people to action.

Adam Przeworski agrees with Thompson in rejecting the idea of class-in-itself and in claiming that the spontaneous organization of class is not permanent: "Classes are not given uniquely by any objective positions because they constitute effects of struggles, and these struggles are not determined uniquely by the relations of production."[8] As with Thompson, class is an effect of struggles that are structured by economic, political, and ideological conditions. Class is a process whereby the effects of struggles mold people into classes and class struggle itself alters the conditions of class formation. Social relations set limits on class development and are themselves limited by class development.

Przeworski opines for methodological individualism, the antithesis of methodological collectivism. Methodological collectivism is a belief that aggregate entities (classes) precede the individual components. This belief sacrifices the individual and poses a logically incoherent view of history. Methodological individualism, however, does not assume class positions and therefore analyzes structures of choice as given to individuals, not to a class. This theory recognizes the fact that individuals may choose to become workers and yet cooperate with capitalists against other workers. Class structure is based on relations of production combined with political and ideological factors. Last, social relations are structures of choice, but they are capable of permutation and are therefore contingent on actions of individuals. Thus, the historian must analyze the entire structure of choice available to individuals.

The issue has therefore shifted to a struggle about class before it is a struggle for class. But how far can one stray from a definition of class based solely on the relations of production without sacrificing the unique merits of Marxist class struggle? Or to restate the question, how closely must a definition of class adhere to the relations of production for it to merit discussion of class struggle? Without the substantive base of class-in-itself, it appears that one could argue that social conflict is a more valid topic of examination than is class conflict. This dilemma was not apparent to Marx because in his time things were progressing as he had theorized: there was a growing proletarianization of the population. Later, though, the size of the working class did indeed stop growing. The realization that a working class based solely on Marx's interpretation of the relations of production would not automatically form a majority forced Marxists to reappraise the organization and mobilization of workers and therefore transcend the simplistic class-in-itself to class-for-itself schema.

6.3 GENDER

Marx, Lenin, and Thompson all agreed that the primary historical actor, or the force that institutes causal change, consists of some form of class. Theories of false consciousness attempt to explain why some people act in a manner inconsistent with their economic class, but perhaps other categories better describe affinities between historical actors such as religious belief, ethnicity, or sex. One is born with a race and sex organs, whereas the categorizations of religious belief, ethnicity, and gender involve culturally contingent notions that are fluid.

Religion is an obvious example of a culturally contingent factor, but what about ethnicity and gender? Biological determinists have sought unsuccessfully to provide scientific explanations for ethnicity. Skin tones vary even within families, so using racial categories to define ethnicity creates definable categories with many people not fitting neatly into a category. Ethnic identity frequently contains racial elements, but it is based on cultural factors and has long ago ceased to be a solely racial distinction.

The sexes, however, are divided into two definable camps with only a fraction of a percentage of biologically ambiguous cases. The biological distinctions have created affinities between individuals of vastly different economic, ethnic, and religious groups. Relations between the sexes constitute a primary element of social organization that is more than a simple derivative of other factors such as class, race, nationality, or religious identity. The fact that individuals readily identify their own gender makes gender a potentially more fruitful category of historical examination than class identity, which may be a product of false class consciousness.

Traditionally, historians focused mainly on male behavior with little consideration of females. This was especially true of political and diplomatic historians in the nineteenth century. Early women's history challenged the male predominance by exploring the history of women who had previously been neglected in historical accounts. The rediscovery of women as historical actors involved new analysis of historical fragments overlooked by male-dominated culture as well as a revisiting of male material from a woman's point of view. Biological distinctions became a ground for creating a new periodization of history, a new focus, and innovative methodology. But to what extent is female behavior biologically or culturally determined? Gender theorists suggest that culturally determined distinctions between men and women are more significant for historical analysis than biological distinctions. Gendered history brings a new vision to history that exceeds the biological distinctions of women's history. Like women's history, it offers a new periodization for history and encourages methodological innovations in order to grasp the category of gender. Furthermore, the focus on culturally determined distinctions between men and women means that gender studies need not be solely about women.

To what extent are differences between men and women culturally determined, and to what extent are they biologically determined?

Sociobiologists emphasize the biological distinctions and conclude that certain kinds of behavior are not culturally determined. For instance, female mammals bear the burden of reproduction, so they need to find a mate that is suitable. Female humans need to be more selective because they need a male who will be neither promiscuous nor absent while the female is reproducing. Sociobiologists claim that natural determinants, such as the stake each of the sexes has in reproduction, are central to creating the male–female distinction.

A spectrum of theories exists between those who view sexual differences as naturally determined and those who see them as socially constructed. Sociobiologists think that much, if not all, sexually linked behavior is determined by nature and in particular by the stake each sex has in reproduction. A similar position is taken by some separatist feminists who view women as different from men because they are superior to men. Mary O'Brien suggests in *The Politics of Reproduction* that men lack a sustained role in reproduction and seek to make up for this deficiency by being more assertive.[9] In other words, patriarchy is an important way for males to become part of reproduction. An entire school of thought accepts sociobiological theories but then argues that the point is not to deny specifically female behavior but to convince society to value it more highly. At the opposite end of the spectrum some feminists emphasize the enormous variety in sexual differences from society to society and subsequently argue that the differences are socially and historically determined.

Adrienne Rich recognizes the sociobiological distinctions and argues that they should be emphasized and given a special role. Lawrence Kohlberg, however, claims that children go through three stages of development with six corresponding stages of moral development. The sense of morality maintaining equilibrium begins very personalized and then matures to "higher" stages where abstract concepts such as "justice" become more apparent. Kohlberg emphasizes the process of moral thought instead of actual control of behavior or the outcome of moral decisions. He concludes that boys advance more quickly and thoroughly through these moral stages.

Carol Gilligan, an educational psychologist who studied the moral development of children, turned Kohlberg upside down by questioning the premise that "abstract" morality is somehow higher and more advanced than the personal sphere of morality. This personal sphere, or interdependent moral self, is relative to the situations one encounters and is thus gender specific. The problem with this entire line of research is that the lack of consensus among specialists makes applications to historical analysis difficult because opponents need merely reject the theoretical presuppositions. A second problem is that if one believes that men and women are the same then one would apply the same standards to each, whereas if one assumes that they are different then comparing women to standards set by men would be unfair.

Most scholars of gender have avoided this quagmire and turned instead to analysis of the cultural and social determinants of gender. The field of gendered studies has itself evolved rapidly from its origins in the study of women's history to more recent analysis of gender constructions that encompass females and males. The earliest historians of women's history took extreme positions focusing on women in order to bring women back into "herstory." These attempts to correct an imbalance in the male-centered accounts of history largely added women to the topics of history without changing the nature of history. The result was a new camp within the study of history that continuously emphasized the marginalization of women and the fact that women had not played a strong role in history. History became "herstory" as women were tacked onto the schema of groups that historians analyzed. The failure to unite the history of women and nonwomen suggested a need to change the very categories of history.

The focus on women's own lives and accomplishments moved women from the footnotes of history but did little to challenge the old ways of writing history. A new field of history evolved when historians began to write about women's experiences and treat them as the focus of historical writing, rather than just adding women to men's history. This new field expressed women's experience on their own terms. Distinctions between old-fashioned "important" activities, like diplomacy and statecraft, and "mere" women's affairs ceased to exist.

Judith Walkowitz's *Prostitution and Victorian Society* provides a vivid example of some benefits to women's history.[10] Walkowitz studied the Contagious Diseases Acts in garrison towns. The acts obliged women suspected of being prostitutes to submit to compulsory genital examinations for venereal disease. This requirement gave a great deal of power to a select group of men who could arrest any woman looking like a prostitute and then lock her up if she did have venereal disease. Intense lobbying on the part of a broad coalition of British women from a wide range of economic classes brought an end to the laws. The laws themselves therefore managed to mobilize women as women, regardless of their class, religion, or other features that separated them. Such campaigns would obviously be incomprehensible without gender as a category of historical analysis. Gender provides a meaningful framework for something clearly gendered such as the Contagious Diseases Acts, but what about less obvious classifications?

Claudia Koonz's analysis of women during Hitler's Third Reich attempts to make women into a category of special importance to the Nazi regime.[11] Koonz examined Nazi women's organizations and complicity in order to show that women were active participants in the persecution of Jews and other minorities. The Nazi separation of spheres of activity placed women at home (*Kinder, Kirche, Küche*). One problem with this approach is that, although female complicity with the Nazi regime existed, the lack of comparative analysis fails to reveal if women's participation was more acute than for those in Franco's Spain or Vichy France. The lack of a comparative perspective weakens the argument, as does Koonz's omission of the fact that labor shortages of the late 1930s provided more and more women an entrance into the German workplace. This increase in women workers happened in spite of Nazi claims to keep women at home.

Beyond these shortcomings, Koonz's thesis faces a major problem in that she does not show that these women acted differently than men; hence, gender as a category contributes little unless she can show that gender was significant. In fact, she fails to demonstrate that gender as such had any particular importance for the Nazi regime, or that women were singled out as a group anymore than by all sorts of conservative regimes elsewhere during the same period. Koonz does offer a refreshing perspective on the Third Reich that is a significant contribution to general historiography despite these shortcomings in terms of gendered history.

Bonnie Anderson and Judith Zinsser's *A History of Their Own* brings to fruition the notion that gender is a crucial category for understanding the past.[12] Their examination of European history through the prism of gender destroys the traditional periodization of the past and offers new periodizations such as England's tradition of female rule. The vantage point of women provides a new perspective on events and thereby forces historians to reconsider widely accepted interpretations. For instance, the ancien régime in France is traditionally seen as a period of virtually no freedoms that was ended by the liberation of the Enlightenment and the Revolution, yet for some women it was a period of greater freedom than what followed. Conversely periods of great liberation such as the Renaissance, the Enlightenment, or Industrialization brought waves of nefarious consequences for women. Renaissance scientific investigation confirmed inherited prejudices about the innate physical inferiority of women, and the Industrial Revolution brought leisure to middle-class women while simultaneously imprisoning them in gilded cages of domesticity and depriving them of the pleasures of work and participation in the public sphere.

Recent reappraisals of historical periodization owe much to Joan Kelly's essay "Did Women Have a Renaissance?"[13] Kelly opened the essay by challenging historians to rethink accepted conventions of periodization. Her first book examined the Renaissance writer Leon Battista Alberti (1404–1472) and the question of perspective. Just as Renaissance art presented new perspectives and vantage points, Kelly posed new historical perspectives and vantage points. Noting Leonardo's comments about how the earth appears from the perspective of the moon, she said:

> All I had done was to say, with Leonardo, suppose we look at the dark, dense immobile earth from the vantage point of the moon? Suppose we look again at this age, the Renaissance, reputed for its liberation from old confining forms, renowned for its revival of classical and republican ideas? Suppose we look at the Renaissance from the vantage point of women?[14]

The women's vantage point exploded previous understanding about women in history and forced a reordering of the past:

> As soon as we take the emancipation of women as our vantage point, we discover that events which change the course of history for men, liberating them from natural, social, or ideological restraints upon their powers, may have quite different, even opposite effects upon women.[15]

Kelly transformed the way historians viewed the past by analyzing women's economic and political roles, the prevailing ideology about women, women's cultural role in shaping society, and the regulation of female sexuality relative to male sexuality. She destroyed the last remnant of teleological history by dispelling the notion that Western civilization had moved from repressive to more liberating structures.

Kelly's work is rooted in a Marxist-feminist analysis with a real focus on consciousness. Her analysis of ideology purports to seek social conditions:

> The sexual nature of courtly love . . . represents an ideological liberation of [feudal women's] sexual and affective powers that must have some social reference. This is not to raise the fruitless question of whether such love relationships actually existed or if they were literary conventions. The real issue regarding ideology is, rather, what kind of society could posit as a social ideal a love relation outside of marriage, one that women freely entered and that, despite its reciprocity, made women the gift givers while men did the service. What were the social conditions that fostered these particular conventions rather than the more common ones of female chastity and/or dependence?[16]

In fact, Kelly's solution is found in the economic and political structures instead of the social conditions. The tension between women's oppression and their real power is rooted in the fact that women's control of courtly love reflected "actual power" in medieval aristocracy, but this love functioned as an accommodative ideal that concealed the "tensions between it and other social values" such as patriarchal marriage.

Gender is now included, along with ethnicity and class, as a category of analysis. Women's distinctive relationships to property and production illuminate social conditions and women's role in society, thereby denying a female "natural destiny" and questioning the position and function of women in particular times and places. This challenge to accepted conventions of periodization forced a reevaluation of the notion that Western civilization had moved from repressive to more liberating structures.

6.4 STRUCTURES OF PERCEPTION

Analysis of the social construction of gender poses a serious conundrum for the rational-choice theorists' presuppositions of inherent rationality: if truth and knowledge about sexuality are victims of historicist relativism, then might not rationality also succumb to historicization? Michel Foucault's radical historicization of truth, knowledge, and rationality involved explaining how and why some things are considered true, knowledge, or rational while others are not. He pursued this search by exploring *epistemes*, or the conditions of knowledge within which organized knowledges are structured.

His early *archaeological* works explored the archaeological level of linguistic structures that defined scientific knowledge but existed beneath human subjectivity. These works questioned scientificity (the state of being scientific) in general by historicizing the emergence of various discourses: reason, unreason, and changing perceptions of madness (*Madness and Civilization*, 1961), the development of clinical medicine (*The Birth of the Clinic*, 1963), and post-Renaissance mutations in the history of sciences (*The Order of Things*, 1966). His next major work, *The Archaeology of Knowledge* in 1969, marked the beginning of a shift from this archaeological approach to *genealogical* analyses of concrete power relations such as his genealogies of penal systems (*Discipline and Punish*, 1975) and Western sexuality (three volumes of *The History of Sexuality*, 1976, 1984, 1986).

Historians have attributed this shift toward the Nietzschean genealogical method to a crisis in left-wing politics, a general paradigm shift in philosophy, and the May 1968 student protests in France. Foucault acknowledged that his examinations of power and the categorization of normal and abnormal were indebted to Nietzsche's analysis of morals, in *On the Genealogy of Morals*, based on historical and cultural factors. Foucault's archaeological and genealogical approaches, as well as his general application of historical methods, had such an influence on contemporary historians that the writing of history in the 1990s became in many ways a forum for proponents, opponents, and modifiers of Foucaultian history.

Foucault focused this archaeology of knowledge on what he termed truth games, or occasions when the subject itself became an object of knowledge. He analyzed two ways that the subject was posited as such an object: as a living subject within the *human sciences* in the seventeenth and eighteenth centuries (*The Order of Things*) and as an insane, ill, or delinquent individual at the opposite end of the normative distribution (*The History of Madness, The Birth of the Clinic,* and *Discipline and Punish*). Foucault's late works focused on sexuality as an example of the history of *subjectivity* whereby the subject is caught in a social construction that makes the subject an object of truth games. For instance he looks at the nineteenth-century rise of a discourse on homosexuality that appeared in psychiatry, jurisprudence, and other fields. This discourse enabled the spread of social controls over homosexual acts, "but it also made possible a *reverse* discourse whereby homosexuality began to speak in its own behalf."[17]

Foucault did not pursue ultimate truths or place of origin; hence he avoided a teleological history of human purpose. His *social construction* of truths and the analysis of configurations, instead of origins, allowed him to emphasize differences that were not evident within the historical framework of teleological development and progress. As with Joan Kelly, this new focus was also indifferent to the existing historical periodization. For instance, the social construction of sexuality and gender suggests that human nature is not a fixed given. Foucault was interested not in the common issue of whether original human nature exists, but rather in how the conceptualization of human nature has functioned in our society. This pursuit of configurations, instead of the traditional origins, is part of his method of historicizing abstractions and universals without seeking recourse to other universals. Noam Chomsky, in contrast, uses human nature as a standard against which society could be judged because he wants to formulate a more humane and just society. Foucault had no notion of an ideal social model and therefore rejected these utopian abstractions. This fact does not diminish the social importance of his message because an understanding of how power actually operates provides an incentive to alter existing power relations.

To understand how power actually operates, "one needs to be nominalistic, no doubt" because "power is not an institution, and not a structure; neither is it a certain strength we are endowed with; it is the name that one attributes to a complex strategical situation in a particular society."[18] Power in society is everywhere. It is not something possessed and controlled by an elite group, as some Marxists contend; it is more like a tattered dollar bill passed endlessly from a diamond-studded money clip to a tattered pocket and back again. Materialist explanations thus cannot fully explain social change for Foucault.

The emphasis on power coincided with a shift in Foucault's work, occurring in 1968, from the unconscious perceptual structures of his archaeological works to a Nietzschean genealogical approach that highlighted concrete power relations. For instance, both *The Birth of the Clinic* (1963) and *Discipline and Punish* (1975) focus on scientific discourse about the body in France during the eighteenth and nineteenth centuries, but the archaeological early work contains virtually no narrative line, whereas the later work employs a clear narrative with explicit references to dates and places. This change occurred not because punishment and penal systems are more conducive to narrative than clinical medicine, but rather because the focus on linguistic structures defining clinical medicine is not as explicit as that on the concrete power relations of penal practices and institutions. This narrative is radically different from the inevitable progress of nineteenth-century grand narratives because Foucault emphasized the petty causes of penal evolution. His rethinking of the past moved the marginal, the social deviants, to the center of a history of discourse about the normal and abnormal. His genealogical approach becomes a self-critical history of the present by including the recovery of what has been forgotten in order to destroy notions of inevitable progress and to emphasize the extent to which mental boundaries constrain society.

This presentist facet runs throughout Foucault's work but is most obvious in his later work on sexuality. He plotted his own work on three axes: a *truth axis* evident in the archaeological works *The Birth of the Clinic* and *The Order of Things*, a *power axis* in the genealogical *Discipline and Punish*, and an *ethical axis* in the three-volume *The History of Sexuality*. Foucault defined *ethics*, the third axis, as "the kind of relationship you ought to have with yourself."[19] The archaeological pursuit of structural truths gave way to a genealogical, poststructural analysis of power and ultimately an ethics that is profoundly presentist because it reveals the extent to which people are victims of power. Professional discourse about abnormal behavior creates mental boundaries that constrain all of society. Moreover, because power is passed endlessly, even the winners are eventual losers. The idea that authority and subversion participate in this cycle of exchange is unacceptable to most proponents of rational-choice, class, or gender analysis of history because blame cannot be placed on concrete notions such as capital or patriarchy.

The four examples of possible historical actors discussed in this chapter may be fashionable at present, but they are not the only possible focal points of analysis. The type of history one wishes to write will influence how one defines historical actors. Other historical actors include status, racial, political, religious, or any other group identity to which individuals feel allegiance or affinity. The very definition of a historical group is problematic because people may not perceive of themselves in the same categories that others perceive them. Boundaries become crucial because defining historical actors involves delineating members of one group from nonmembers. Categories, be they universal or local, require exclusions and thus the rejection of certain perspectives.

Historians obviously need to emphasize the role of certain historical actors over others, but no professional consensus exists as to the best choice. One contemporary critic has concluded that we need to "explore new topics" because we "cannot afford simply to keep recounting the same narratives of class, race and gender, indispensable as these topics are."[20] The most fashionable current trend has been for historians to consider the postcolonialist focus on the margins or borders of a category (see the discussion of hybridity and the subaltern in Chapter 8). Ultimately the choice becomes a question of artistic sensibility derived from experience, presuppositions, and the desire to tell a certain type of history.

NOTES

1. Mancur Olson, *The Logic of Collective Action* (Cambridge, MA: Harvard University Press, 1965).

2. Ibid., p. 108.

3. Garrett Hardin, "The Tragedy of the Commons: The Population Problem Has No Technical Solution; It Requires a Fundamental Extension in Morality," *Science* 162 (1968): 1243–1248.

4. Karl Marx, *The Poverty of Philosophy*, introduction by Frederick Engels (New York: International Publishers, 1963), p. 173.

5. E. P. Thompson, *The Making of the English Working Class* (New York: Random House, 1963), p. 11.

6. Ibid.

7. Ibid., p. 13.

8. Adam Przeworski, "Proletariat into a Class: The Process of Class Formation," in A. Przeworski (ed.), *Capitalism and Social Democracy* (Cambridge: Cambridge University Press, 1985), p. 66, see also pp. 67–71.

9. Mary O'Brien, *The Politics of Reproduction* (Boston: Routledge & Kegan Paul, 1981).

10. Judith Walkowitz, *Prostitution and Victorian Society* (Cambridge: Cambridge University Press, 1980).

11. Claudia Koonz, *Mothers in the Fatherland: Women, the Family, and Nazi Politics* (New York: St. Martin's Press, 1987).

12. Bonnie S. Anderson and Judith P. Zinsser, *A History of Their Own: Women in Europe from Prehistory to the Present* (New York: Harper & Row, 1988).

13. Joan Kelly, "Did Women Have a Renaissance?," in *Women, History and Theory: The Essays of Joan Kelly* (Chicago: University of Chicago Press, 1984), pp. 19–50.

14. Ibid., p. xiii.

15. Ibid., p. 19.

16. Ibid., p. 26.

17. Michel Foucault, *The History of Sexuality, volume 1: An Introduction* (New York: Vintage Books, 1980, © 1978), p. 101.

18. Ibid., p. 93. See pp. 92–102 for Foucault's description of power.

19. Foucault discussed this topic in 1983 interviews with Paul Rabinow and Hubert Dreyfus that were published as *Michel Foucault: Beyond Structuralism and Hermeneutics* (eds.), Dreyfus and Rabinow, 2nd edn. (Chicago: University of Chicago Press, 1983).

20. Terry Eagleton, *After Theory* (New York: Basic Books, 2003), p. 222.

Chapter *7*

Postmodernist (Re)Visions

Content that you finally have a grasp on the history of the absent roommate, you head home to read the assignment for your morning English class. The title catches your attention: "Postmodernism and the Rise of the New Historicists." The term "postmodernism" comes from "postmodern" architecture that rejects the technological abstractions of modernist architecture and claims to be like historical allusions, eclectic and whimsical. Postmodern philosophy is a form of skepticism that recognizes that knowledge does not simply reflect reality; it creates this reality in the process of knowing it. Postmodern philosophy emphasizes language as one of the constituent elements of reality. The result is that there is no objective reality or objective truth, simply relativistic truths and reality. Reality suddenly becomes like Thomas Kuhn's knowledge: something determined by the paradigm (see Section 3.1).

The reading becomes too obtuse, and you suddenly get the idea that the writer is consciously proud of the ability to be obscure and difficult to understand. You skip ahead to the New Historicists and discover that they are in fact removing the distinction between historical and literary materials. The "true" past cannot be reconstructed because it is contingent on the vantage point of those seeking it. In other words, they acknowledge that their interpretations have a presentist bias, so they proudly display their politics. Lee Patterson goes so far as to say,

> The question is not whether we are going to engage in a politically charged critical activity or not. It is, rather, to recognize that since all forms of criticism are evidently and by definition political, which form we choose to practice is an act with consequences.[1]

The New Historicists return to historical context with an awareness of anthropological and sociological studies. Self-conscious critics need to examine literature and the reception of that literature within its own context. Kuhn's historicism of science is joined with an extreme historicism of literature, reception, culture, and theory. The New Historicists reject the metanarratives of a victorious nation-state and champion the centrality of historical knowledge.

7.1 HISTORY AND/AS LANGUAGE

7.1.1 Semiotics and Poststructuralism

French structuralism influenced literary theory and the writing of history in significant ways. Ferdinand de Saussure's analysis of the structure of language privileged the spoken word over the written word because signifiers (words) only have meaning within a network of a language (signs). Cultural expressions such as literature are understood within the preexisting structures of a language. The structure of a language exists prior to the creation of a new word or signifier. Each mental concept (signified) corresponds to a signifier (word), but a word can have more than one meaning (more than one signified). In spoken communication, nonverbal clues help one to understand more precisely and thus spoken communication is better than written communication.

Roland Barthes reversed this and claimed that written formats (signifier) could precede the actual concept (signified). For instance, early speakers of a language may have looked at cave drawings before creating a concept. Images on the wall of a cave depicting animals being hunted in a precise geographical location, such as the bend of a nearby river or a portion of a specific valley, could have given rise to the concept of hunting grounds before the actual phrase was uttered. The written text (signifier) is thus more important than the verbal concept (signified). Barthes severed the connection between the author's conception of reality and the text that the author produced. He called his method semiology, or the science of signs.

One advantage that Barthes's written work holds over the writings of his contemporary structuralists and poststructuralists is that his writing is very accessible to a wide audience. His book *Mythologies* (1957) is a collection of short essays that explore cultural phenomena as diverse as professional wrestling and French wines. His analysis of professional wrestling offers an example of how cultural myths structure knowledge. The rules of professional wrestling and boxing are very different in terms of the actual rules as well as the expected implementation of those rules. Boxing rules exist to limit what the combatants do inside the ring and they are enforced carefully. The rules for wrestling are real but they are enforced in a manner that allows for rules to be broken. Viewers expect some wrestlers to employ forbidden maneuvers (signs) and the audience participates with the wrestlers in the dramatic unfolding of a moral story about justice or the struggle between good and evil (the signified). Boxing is a sport where the winner is decided based on the performance during the fight. Professional wrestling on the other hand is a staged event that is fixed. Spectators will bet heavily on boxing but never on wrestling. Yet wrestling has a wide viewership because the audience understands the myth that frames the wrestling match. The myth of social justice is embodied in the wrestling match. The immediate myth of the wrestling match, with all of its staged fighting, is only understood within a larger cultural myth of social justice.

Beyond introducing the cultural role of myths, Barthes also shifted the focus from the speaker or author to the actual text that was created. Instead of analyzing the intentions of the speaker or author, one now analyzes the logic of the written text. The author's intentions are unknowable so the scholar focuses instead on the logic of the text. The "death of the author" simply means that the author is dead to analysis because analysis is now solely of the text. Barthes, along with Michel Foucault, moved us beyond the assumption that archival knowledge will allow us to reconstruct reality. The structure of language required a deconstruction, or analysis of the logic of the text with no consideration of the intentions of the author or subject. Some people consider this the origin of deconstruction while others attribute the origin to Derrida at a slightly later time. Structuralists used linguistics in order to inventory the logically possible word combinations and thus the logic of a text. Foucault's social construction of knowledge and Barthes's semiotics are transitional moves toward poststructuralism because the focus shifted from the linguistic structure to the logic of the specific text. Instead of analyzing the text as a product of a linguistic system the text itself came to be viewed as its own system.

7.1.2 Deconstruction

Jacques Derrida proclaimed the beginning of deconstruction, and the end of structuralism, in 1966 when he presented the paper "Structure, Sign, and Play in the Discourse of the Human Sciences" to a conference at Johns Hopkins University. This despite the fact that structuralism at that time was gaining popularity in many fields beyond linguistics. Ferdinand de Saussure's treatment of language as structure suggested that the meaning of a text could best be understood by structural analysis. His description of the arbitrary relationship between signifiers, or words that designate an idea or concept, and the signified, the actual idea or concept, meant that the meaning of words derives from other words and not from reference to reality. Because words have meaning relative to other words, structuralist linguists examine systems of signifiers synchronically, or at one given time, whereas philologists and historical linguists examine the diachronic, historical development of words. If structuralists could study language as a structure, then certainly other cultural practices could also be analyzed in the same fashion.

Derrida's attack was actually against anthropologist Claude Lévi-Strauss's structural analysis of nature (universal) and culture (norms varying from one social structure to another). Lévi-Strauss studied the "elemental structures of kinship" by analyzing kinship systems as permutations of the same fundamental elements, for example, the binary oppositions between male and female. But the "incest taboo" posed the greatest challenge to him because it was universal and also part of the system of norms. The taboo's status as nature and culture challenged his assumptions of a nature/culture dichotomy. Derrida dismissed Lévi-Strauss's entire system of thought because this contradiction undermines its foundation: the nature/culture system was deconstructed, not destroyed, by "taking it to pieces" and showing the contradictions upon which it is based.

Derrida's deconstruction shows the instability of meaning in general as he expands his critique to Western philosophy and logic. We express ourselves in opposites such as beginning/end, presence/absence, and construction/destruction. Moreover, these opposites or dichotomies contain hierarchical orderings whereby one term is superior and the other inferior. For instance, speech is privileged because it is based on the speaker's presence, whereas writing is inferior because it is based on the absence of the writer. A word's meaning is relative to other words, according to Ferdinand de Saussure; hence, all meanings are contingent on differences between words. Language is constituted by differences or, as Derrida explains, by *la différance* (Derrida's neologism from the verb *différer* suggests both differ and defer). All texts can be read in different ways (*la différence*) and exhaustive interpretation is forever deferred (*la différance*). In *Dissemination*, Derrida tracks Western logocentrism to Plato and then shows how Plato's own text dismantled Platonism when Socrates condemned writing in *Phaedrus*.[2] Socrates did not leave any written texts, and his championing of speaking over writing is known only because Plato chose to write it. Moreover, Socrates made his point about the superiority of speaking by reference to metaphors about writing. In so doing, he invoked the power of writing while attempting to displace it from the center to the margin. Might not speaking thus be said to be a secondary form of writing? The deconstruction of this and all other texts was possible because the text itself contained the seeds of its own refutation.

Derrida is pleased with structuralism's demystification of the metaphysical, but he argues that it makes claims for something that is more than arbitrary: if structuralists could do what they claimed, then they would create a "ghost town" in that the spirit would be fully removed. They destroy the metaphysical center upon which most of Western thought is constructed. Derrida applauds this destruction but rejects Western logocentrism and structuralist attempts to explain laws governing human signification because they are based on assumed centers or ideal meanings. In the end, he is left with the instability of meaning in general because the only language available to discuss philosophy is language inherited from philosophy (just as the only way we know to think about nature and culture involves making the distinction between the two). We have no language that is alien to this philosophical history; hence, the deconstructers' own discourse is just as subject to deconstruction as anyone else's discourse.

7.1.3 Postmodernism

Postmodern philosophy and poststructuralism appear to pride themselves on deliberate obscurity. Their penchant for obfuscation is consistent with a deeper intolerance for authority. Postmodernists embrace a radical form of skepticism and then elevate it to a general belief denying that one objective reality exists. This rejection of objective truth produces a relativistic outlook that is equally suspicious of any attempted "master narrative" in terms of which human society or history is understood. The rejection of master narratives is a rejection of totalizing philosophies that rely on narratives such as Enlightenment thought in general, Hegel, and the Christian tradition.

Postmodernists look to Nietzsche, Wittgenstein, and the long tradition of skeptical philosophy that denies qualities and hierarchies of knowledge such as those existing in the science-versus-art debate in Chapter 1. Knowledge mirrors what is out there, but the existence of reciprocal influences between the observer and nature means that knowledge does not just reflect reality; it actually creates a new reality in the process of knowing it. Similar to Kuhn's description of paradigms determining knowledge, postmodernism's skeptical philosophy denies the existence of objective, universal truths.

The term "postmodernism" comes from a school of architecture that rejects the sleek, technological abstraction of modernist architecture. Postmodern philosophy stands as the culmination of a long tradition of skeptical philosophy that has shown us the extent to which knowledge does not just reflect reality, but creates this reality in the process of knowing it. The novelty of postmodern philosophy is an emphasis on language as one of the constituent elements of reality.

In "Reworking the Past," Section 3.3, we examined the role of language in mediating knowledge and determining reality. Postmodernists such as Jacques Derrida completely severed any connection between reality and the text because language itself determined reality. A word's meaning was determined by its reference to other words instead of to reality. This separation of text from reality means that the author plays no privileged role in the interpretation of texts. We summarized three important implications that postmodernist notions of language had for history: (1) the disappearance of the author and the historical actor as a coherent subject, (2) the disappearance of the text as something with a unique discernible meaning, and (3) the disappearance of any teleology in history. Postmodernists show us the extent to which subjectivist, rhetorical, and literary biases influence the writing of history.

Joan Scott's feminist attack on historical categorization is not in itself postmodern, but it contributed in subtle ways to postmodern abandonment of previously accepted historical tools and methods. Her call for a new chronology of history challenged the patriarchal bias of commonly accepted categories of historical periodization. But Scott also rejected the existence of any essential nature that is male or female because such notions are historically produced and are contingent on sexual identities.

This rejection of inherent essences, such as being *male* or *female*, frees historians from accepted categories and thus allows them to create new and more useful categories. Moreover, Scott's attack on Gilligan's theory of female justice as the perpetuation of stereotypes with ahistorical models forces gender historians to legitimate their descriptions of gender as historically specific. The general questioning and discarding of categorization poses an intriguing dilemma because it simultaneously liberates historians from existing categories and threatens to abandon all tools that historians have developed and relied upon.

Postmodernist tendencies and applications have influenced the writing of history both in subtle ways, such as Scott's work, and in consciously bold ways. The notion of language as constituent reality was a guiding assumption of Gareth Stedman Jones's *Languages of Class*.[3] He looked at the language of Chartism and found no economic or social reason to expand suffrage. Language in this analysis is not just a reflection of the past but in fact a constituent part of the past. To remain engaged in discussions of the past, historians, be they postmodern or not, are therefore forced to be cognizant of new tools of analysis so that they may choose to incorporate or critique the postmodern analysis of the past.

The emphasis of literary theory on the study of texts has led some historians to abandon history as the study of the past and emphasize historical studies as literary text. Hayden White champions the role of language to such an extent that the paradigm shifts from history of language to history as language. White's *Metahistory* views the historical text as a literary artifact.[4] The very title, derived from "metaphysics," or the contemplation of that which is beyond the physical, suggests something beyond history. The examination of historical texts as literary artifacts erases the distinction between history and story.

But this distinction may have more to do with the English language than with an accurate description of ultimate differences between history and story. The dichotomy does not exist in most other European languages, as *Geschichte* equals *Geschichte*, *storia* equals *storia*, and *histoire* equals *histoire*. Histories after all evolved out of the chronicles. The chronicles listed facts, and history took the facts and turned them into a story. The writing of history relies on literary techniques such as the use of beginnings and ends with some form of plot in the middle. History requires emplotment, as the facts are manipulated into a plot structure. Historians turn facts into stories that fit established genres such as tragedy, comedy, romance, or realism. The events themselves may be value neutral, but any telling of the events involves choices of plot and emphasis that are not value neutral.

7.2 SOCIOHISTORICAL PURSUIT AND THE RISE OF THE NEW HISTORICISM

In the middle of the twentieth century, American literary criticism was largely dominated by close textual analysis known as the New Criticism. The New Critics treated texts as aesthetic objects filled with complicated meanings that were not discernible by analysis of historical intentions and authorial circumstances. Critical interpretations of text replaced historical and philological scholarship, as the primary task of literary knowledge shifted from scholarship to criticism. Beginning in the late 1960s, a wide range of theoretical issues from other fields of inquiry, such as structuralism, Marxism, psychoanalysis, feminism, and eventually deconstruction, posed a serious challenge to the New Criticism's hegemony.

One group, calling themselves the New Historicists, samples from this smorgasbord of new theories but with a discerning palate: they accept materialist considerations without the pure class conflict of the Marxists; they embrace deconstruction's instability of meaning but maintain a smattering of American philosophical pragmatism; they employ anthropological perspectives of local knowledge from the native's point of view while remaining self-conscious of their own status as interpreters; and they focus on Foucault's power, knowledge, and overlapping causation, yet they are not obsessed with the archaeological. Thus they fail to embrace fully any of these four trends, opting instead to draw on aspects of each while simultaneously expanding the New Critics' prescription of close textual analysis. They emphasize the textuality of history and thus make history itself the object of interpretation, or, as New Historicist Louis Montrose defined it, the "reciprocal concern with the historicity of texts and the textuality of history."

This intentional reintroduction of historical factors into literary theory differs from the early twentieth-century emphasis on historical facts and events because the New Historicists acknowledge that historical reality is in part created through interpretations of historical texts. Brook Thomas has pointed out that "the coupling of 'new' with historicism is redundant" because "historicism, a product of the modern imagination, assumes that history will always be made new."[5] The New Historicists avoid the totalizing determinism of nineteenth-century German historicism, and they try to avoid the organicism of earlier combinations of history and literature whereby critics scoured a text for virtually every fundamental idea of a specific era.

The *new* aspect of the New Historicism involves the juxtaposition of literary and nonliterary texts combined with the insistence that nonliterary texts should be *read* with the same vigor that is applied to traditional literary texts. The required deeper reading of these nonliterary texts thus turns them into more than mere factual documents. It also involves application of interdisciplinary methods, specifically borrowing from Foucault, Derrida, and anthropologist Clifford Geertz. The New Historicists identify regulatory practices and the historical functioning of discourse (Foucault), decenter the study of history (Derrida), and recognize their own historical position as interpreter (Geertz). The infusion of Geertz's innovative methodology includes employment of a thick description, whereby cultural fragments such as cockfighting in Bali provide a microcosm of the entire culture, recognition of culturally and historically specific *local knowledge* and, most importantly, the self-conscious recognition of their own role as critics viewing a different set of cultural values.

Drawing on Marxism, Derrida, Foucault, Geertz, and others, the New Historicists reveal how works of literature simultaneously influence and are influenced by the broader culture. Literary texts thus absorb and refashion social and cultural energy. Like the passage of the tattered dollar bill, used in Chapter 6 to explain Foucault's notion of power, the process of circulation and exchange between literary texts and culture can be tracked and analyzed. And a good tracker can follow these spurs, or tracks, to various cultural conflicts out of which written records are generated. These trackers are not interested in some literary canon's purported cultural heritage, opting instead to search for literary texts that offer the most intriguing remnants of cultural conflict.

The infusion of new theoretical considerations into analysis of texts, combined with a postmodern historicism that is self-admittedly presentist, has opened new connections between writing history and literary criticism. The rise of a New Historicism within literature departments coupled with the rise of a new cultural history within history departments has produced "the common ground of cultural studies for both historians and literary critics discontent with particular constraints within their respective disciplines."[6] Thick description, the distinguishing between a wink and a blink based on the perspective of local knowledge, allowed the New Historicists a hermeneutic for disentangling texts without recourse to class struggle or macroeconomic change.

Nevertheless, market relations and capitalism have a profound influence on art and life, and the New Historicists tend to focus on the market's distorting effects on people and artistic representations. The early New Historicists focused on Renaissance topics, and their treatment of nascent capitalism was less than positive: the capitalist shift from status to contract created hollow, empty personalities that resembled money itself. The heresy of good capitalism is evident in Greenblatt's claim that "society's dominant currencies, money and prestige, are invariably involved."[7] In his *Shakespearean Negotiations*, Greenblatt proposes that all aesthetic representation anticipates or embodies market relations.

One can debate whether New Historicist strategies are actually consistent with liberatory politics, but the more significant issue for historians is whether the writing of history is an arbitrary and illogical business. The New Historicists' self-consciousness about the poetics, or literary conventions, of their own work and their attempts to peel away fictive elements from historical texts have profound implications for the writing of history. The heightened awareness of narrative and rhetorical practices in the construction of texts poses two significant challenges for historians: first, consideration of how historical documents were constructed and, second, a self-conscious consideration of the forms of representation that we as historians employ. Neither of these is new, but Hayden White's earlier challenge takes on a new significance because the New Historicists (1) show how the application of literary criticism reveals a rhetoric of documents, and (2) themselves experiment with their own representations in a manner that blurs traditional boundaries between fact and fiction. For instance, any writing based on recurrent plot structures contains a fictive element created by the plotting of a beginning, a middle, and an end.

7.3 THE CULTURAL TURN

The phrase "cultural turn" appeared in the title of a 1998 book by Fredric Jameson (*The Cultural Turn: Selected Writings on the Postmodern, 1983–1998*) and of a 1999 volume edited by Victoria Bonnell and Lynn

Hunt (*Beyond the Cultural Turn: New Directions in the Study of Society and Culture*). That this turn to analysis of culture has influenced the writing of history is evident in the publication in the past decade of many introductions to cultural history. Peter Burke's *What Is Cultural History?* (2005) has already been reissued in a second edition (2008) and remains one of the best introductions to the field. James W. Cook has gone so far as to question the coupling of "turn" with cultural history in an *American Historical Review* article entitled "The Kids Are All Right: On the 'Turning' of Cultural History" (June 2012). Cook reminds us that cultural history was a vibrant field prior to the construction of the term cultural turn. The act of writing these overviews to cultural history allows the field to be better defined and understood, but also suggests that cultural history has become so conventional that it is no longer the newest trend in writing history.

The origins of the "cultural turn" are complicated. For the purposes of this introduction the origins may be designated as (1) the "metahistory" of Hayden White, (2) French structuralism and poststructuralism (Roland Barthes, Michel Foucault, and Jacques Derrida), (3) cultural geography (Clifford Geertz), and (4) Marxist social history that included analysis of culture (Edward P. Thompson). The New Historicists, with their focus on cultural representations, were part of the cultural turn and they drew heavily on the four traditions. Hayden White's 1973 book *Metahistory: The Historical Imagination in Nineteenth-Century Europe* and Clifford Geertz's 1973 collection of essays entitled *The Interpretation of Culture* are two works that Victoria Bonnell and Lynn White pinpoint as the most influential books in starting the cultural turn. Bonnell and White follow Geoff Eley in referring to White as the "patron saint" of the cultural turn. White was certainly important in the blossoming of cultural history and specifically the tendency among cultural historians to be self-reflexive about the writing of history. This self-reflexive writing of history includes recognition of the limits of plot (the creation of a beginning, a middle and an end of a history), the construction of a historical narrative, and the recognition that judgments about the past are not value free. White's *Metahistory* and his *Tropics of Discourse: Essays in Cultural Criticism* (1978) were important contributions to contemporary understandings of the relationship between history and narrative discourse, specifically the way that tropes, a form of figurative language, constrains what can be said about the past. White also has connections to the ideas of Roland Barthes, especially the relationship of myth to history.

Ferdinand de Saussure's structuralism claimed that meaning was to be found in a sign's difference from other signs. The structure of one language differed from that of another language and thus one culture can be understood by its difference from other cultures. Barthes's focus on semiotics and myths also encouraged analysis of how one culture differed from another. This offered historians an opportunity to explore symbols and rituals as meaningful topics. Geertz's thick description and analysis from the native's point of view allowed one to see cockfighting as a sentimental education for inhabitants of Bali. Barthes's focus on myths and the science of society's signs allowed one to demystify things in culture that appear commonplace and to show how even the mundane is historically contingent. Culture for both involved analyzing social functions and exploring values that are evident in events as banal as wrestling matches and cockfighting. One consistency of Geertz's and Barthes's was that a synchronic understanding of culture allows one to understand the wrestling match and cockfighting. The native's point of view, thick description, and the understanding of cultural myths are part and parcel of grasping culture.

Culture itself can be viewed as the values and practices of a group whereby one analyses culture as a group's self-expression. But culture can also be viewed as something that is imposed on a people. British social historians of the 1960s and 1970s began to analyze popular culture to explore how ideology was imposed on lower class people. Their interest in the absence of strong class activity (the class-in-itself not becoming class-for-itself) led to a search for ways in which our decisions are influenced by forces beyond our control such as ideology. Edward P. Thompson's influential book *The Making of the English Working Class* (1963) examined shared experiences and ideologies that were not economic. Thompson strayed from the traditional materialist focus on economic relations of production and the Marxist categories of base and superstructure. He drew on the works of Antonio Gramsci, an early twentieth-century Italian Marxist. Gramsci had crafted a theory of cultural hegemony whereby the capitalist state maintains power by controlling culture and ideology. Thompson's cultural materialism saw culture as indispensable and irreducible. Culture encodes economic concerns and thus becomes the lynchpin of analysis. Thompson resisted being considered part of the cultural turn, but his works influenced social historians who now turned their focus to questions of culture.

The conflation of these diverse trends in history resulted in a focus on culture that created the cultural turn. The narrative that was just presented, of four traditions merging into the cultural turn, revealed a diachronic unfolding of four overlapping traditions that oversimplified the messy shift to cultural history. This narrative is itself not consistent with the spirit of the cultural turn. Moreover the narrow delineation of the cultural turn misses the broad and often conflicting tendencies of cultural history. The twentieth century ended with heated public discourse about the rise of political correctness, the content of textbooks, and the notion of "culture wars." Culture was suddenly a controversial topic and scholars of diverse ideological and political ilk had a vested interest in engaging culture and its recent history. Cultural studies became a controversial and vibrant field of study in part because it encouraged interdisciplinary opportunities for engaging literary theory, anthropology, art history, sociology, and history. The interdisciplinary nature of cultural studies lent itself to an expansion of cultural history into a field that was previously considered comparative history. Cultural history embraced microscopic analysis of subcultures as well as global comparisons of culture that could be politically controversial.

Some scholars of culture began to examine the hybridity, the mixing of cultures within people, and thus shifted the discussion of otherness to a degree whereby the other could coexist within a culture. Hybridity is best viewed as a montage of diverse cultural influences combined with influences from diverse cultures. The hybrid is the mixture of cultures that influence an individual who exists within a definable culture. Imperialism and postcolonialism both contributed to transcultural forms that consist of a cross-breeding of cultures. Creole is an example of a hybrid language and an international exchange student is an example of hybridity in an academic institution. Culture shifts back and forth from something that exists for, and is imposed on, people to the life experiences of communities full of diverse individuals. Through all of this culture, or the hybridity of cultures, became the focal point of scholarship. The creation and dissemination of high culture was replaced by an examination of both the construction and the experience of popular culture or even marginalized groups. The cultural turn altered the focus of history and opened a new door to global analysis of cultures.

Postmodernism revealed the extent to which historical writing is subject not only to the political biases of historians but also to inherent biases of rhetorical and literary aspects of writing. Some historians are slowly beginning to tolerate and even encourage poetic innovations in the writing of history. The entire postmodernist exercise can be very liberating if the master narratives attacked are oppressive, but the ensuing free-for-all that postmodernism allows may produce some results that are undesirable. The cultural turn certainly changed the scope of history, but it has also revealed the extent to which history misses the voices of some groups. Comparative analysis of cultures has fostered a shift to global comparisons and the rise of new voices of oppression. The shift to global comparisons has also resulted in new directions in the field of postcolonial studies that have profound repercussions on the writing of history.

NOTES

1. Lee Patterson, *Literary Practice and Social Change in Britain, 1380–1530* (Berkeley: University of California Press, 1990), p. 14.

2. Jacques Derrida, *Dissemination*, trans. with an introduction and additional notes, by Barbara Johnson (Chicago: Chicago University Press, 1981).

3. Gareth Stedman Jones, *Languages of Class: Studies in English Working Class History, 1832–1982* (Cambridge/New York: Cambridge University Press, 1983).

4. Hayden White, *Metahistory: The Historical Imagination in Nineteenth-Century Europe* (Baltimore: Johns Hopkins University Press, 1973).

5. Brook Thomas, *The New Historicism and Other Old-Fashioned Topics* (Princeton, NJ: Princeton University Press, 1991), p. 32.

6. Ibid., p. 11.

7. Stephen Greenblatt, *Shakespearean Negotiations* (Berkeley: University of California Press, 1988), p. 12.

Chapter 8

Postcolonialism and the Scope of History

Consider briefly how the disappearance of your roommate has fundamentally altered your understanding of your everyday existence. You once held an unreflective belief that all was basically well between you and your roommate. This belief was shattered when you realized that your roommate was gone. In what philosophers would term an "epistemological crisis," the disappearance undermined a whole set of assumptions. During an epistemological crisis, existing assumptions are dispelled, and one is left grabbing for any new set of assumptions that may explain the situation and thereby make it rational again. The entire roommate episode has been a trying time both emotionally and mentally. At certain points the situation seemed so overwhelming that it prevented you from socializing and making future plans, but you persevered with your study of Western historiography because you believed the past could inform the present and thereby contribute to a new epistemology. Has your new, comprehensive understanding restored rationality to your life, or have you, in a panic, embraced a new set of assumptions that may also be faulty?

The time has come to put the entire incident behind you and get on with your life. It is finally time to ask someone else to become your new roommate. When you pose the question, a telling glimmer in the friend's eye reveals something humorous about your request.

"No . . . ah . . . I already have a roommate for next academic year, but thanks for asking."

What? Why did you not know of the friend's plans? You ask, "So who are you rooming with?"

"Oh, . . . Your old roommate moved in five days ago."

Wow! Another epistemological crisis! Once again your entire set of assumptions has collapsed, and this time they are shattered despite your extensive deliberations about the situation. What does the study of historiography bring you if it allows you to be so mistaken? Has your analysis of the "otherness" of the past taught nothing? Or has this pursuit been part of a peculiarly Western method of essentializing otherness as an object? Why do people define themselves by saying what they are not instead of saying what they are? Postcolonialism offers a harsh critique of Western thought precisely because the West defines itself via this construction of otherness.

Why do you need a roommate to begin with? Can you not live on your own with your own identity? Consider ways in which a roommate has changed you into a hybrid of yourself and the roommate. Your musical and decorative tastes were slightly modified to accommodate those of your former roommate. Even if you were to remove all items that had belonged to your roommate, you would undoubtedly find that remnants of the roommate remain because your apartment is filled with traces of memory that constantly remind you of your shared past.

How should you deal with your post-roommate existence? What part of your previous life should remain and what should go? Do you abandon all music that was neither yours nor your roommate's? What about that hybrid music that the two of you enjoyed precisely because it disturbed the sensibilities of neither of you? Your post-roommate solution may have parallels with academics in postcolonial societies. To what extent should they reject their own education, scholarly language, and other remnants of colonialism? Postcolonialism is in part a postcolonial movement, but it is more than that.

The actual term "postcolonialist" is a rallying label, despite all of its ambiguity, for supporters and opponents. As such, the term is closer to "feminist" than to other labels such as "neo-Marxist," "neo-Functionalist," or "New Historicist." The last three terms are usually not applied by either supporters or opponents with the same strategic effect as the first two terms. Adherents and opponents of postcolonialism and feminism are quick to champion the labels, albeit for radically different strategies. Supporters employ these terms as badges of courage that are proudly displayed in conferences and publications in a unifying manner (we are in this together even if the others want to marginalize us). Adversaries use them in order to exclude or marginalize adherents as unworthy of serious consideration.

Moreover, postcolonialists, much like early feminists, attempt to establish a marginalized group within a discourse that has traditionally focused on an exclusive center. Early examples of both attempted to invert this center–margin dichotomy by constructing a "herstory" or "theirstory" to replace "history" and by establishing a "female" or "marginalized" canon to compete with the "male" canon. Both have since superseded these crude inversions and turned to analysis of the mechanisms that allowed the earlier canon to be constructed. Feminism and postcolonialism thus offer the opportunity to assert ideological tendencies without sacrificing an intellectually defensible pursuit of history.

8.1 HISTORY OF THE TERM "POSTCOLONIALISM"

The related terms "commonwealth" and "Third World" flourished in the *postwar* writing of history, especially within the field of *minority studies*, only to be collectively replaced in the 1990s by the term "postcolonial," or initially by the hyphenated term "post-colonial" and later by the unhyphenated "postcolonial." The third edition of *The American Heritage Dictionary of the English Language* defines "postcolonial" as "of, relating to, or being the time following the establishment of independence in a colony" and offers the example of "postcolonial economies." This emphasis on the temporal character of the word is consistent with the use of the hyphenated term because "post" suggests something behind us. "Post-colonial" in this usage replaces "postwar" in defining historical periodization from a European perspective, marking the departure of the British and French from Africa, India, the Caribbean, and other regions. The unhyphenated form implies a way of framing information. Like the term "postmodern," to which postcolonial thought is clearly indebted, the term "postcolonial" describes a perspective or academic attitude that directs methodology. Postmodern and postcolonial studies both developed from literary studies into a wide range of disciplines with a decidedly cultural focus.

This basic split between time frame (postcolonial) and methodological outlooks (postcolonial) can be further divided into types of time frames and types of outlooks. The time frame may be limited to a literal description of formerly colonial societies, but it has come to include global conditions after colonialism. The actual age of colonialism can be argued to have begun in the sixteenth century, or it can be seen as a timeless trait of human interaction that includes virtually all societies. The broadest of frameworks explores marginality and diaspora in any society. This broad focus is consistent with the methodological definition of postcolonialism as a description of global conditions or, more precisely, the postcolonial description of those conditions. On an intellectual level, this definition would involve understanding how corporate groups exploit other corporate groups throughout history. On a more political level, it examines social asymmetries in any society because "colonialism" suggests political inequalities. For instance, J. Jorge Klor de Alva proposes

> that postcoloniality can best be thought of as a form of contestatory/ oppositional consciousness, emerging from either preexisting imperial, colonial, or ongoing subaltern conditions, which fosters processes aimed at revising the norms and practices of antecedent or still vital forms of domination. . . . In short, postcoloniality is contained both within colonialism, . . . and outside of it, by its questioning of the very norms that establish the inside/outside, oppressor/oppressed binaries that are assumed to characterize the colonial condition.[1]

Postcolonialism is thus more than the study of dependency and control; it is a strategic label that suggests an identification capable of motivating people to create change.

Postcolonialism recognizes that voices of the colonized and the colonizer mix in a form of hybridity that merges the two voices. This hybrid voice is powerful because it has the potential to undermine the colonizer. The focus on hybridity involves more than the mere study of marginality. The center wants an identifiable margin in order to label and control that margin. Hence, many postcolonialists reject the notion of minority studies or multiculturalism as simply an attempt to identify and inhibit a potentially subversive margin. Some critics of multiculturalism claim it calls for a pluralism that forces marginalized people to speak as a proxy for a broader "community" regardless of whether or not the designated speakers share the same socioeconomic status as a majority from that community. Bhiku Parekh's political formulations of multiculturalism also propose community rights, rather than individual rights, which allow no universal human rights but also no right of exit for people born into a group that they dislike. The external other is thus a product of the observers' observations as they silence communal voices by recognizing spokespeople that may not be representative of individuals within that community.

The analysis of hybridity, otherness, and cultural difference is consistent with historians' pursuit of the otherness of the past. Postcolonialism is also consistent with late twentieth-century rejections of universal narratives. In the words of Homi K. Bhabha, one of the leading theorists of hybridity:

> The grand narrative of nineteenth-century historicism on which its claims to universalism were founded—Evolutionism, Utilitarianism, Evangelism—were also, in another textual and territorial time-space, the technologies of colonial and imperialist governance. It is the "rationalism" of these ideologies of progress that increasingly come to be eroded in the encounter with the "contingency" of cultural difference.[2]

The term "post-colonial" became mainstream in 1989 with the publication of *The Empire Writes Back: Theory and Practice in Post-Colonial Literatures* by Bill Ashcroft, Gareth Griffiths, and Helen Tiffin. The authors used "post-colonial" to cover "all the culture affected by the imperial process from the moment of colonization to the present day. This is because there is a continuity of preoccupations throughout the historical process initiated by European imperial aggression."[3] In a 1995 anthology entitled *The Post-Colonial Studies Reader*, the same authors discussed contemporary debates about the term "post-colonialism" and offered a further elaboration of their own definition: (1) an amorphous set of discursive practices, akin to postmodernism; and (2) a more specific, and "historically" located, set of cultural strategies that should not be limited to the period after the colonies became independent because it is more descriptive of the totality of practices, in all their diversity, which characterize the societies of the postcolonial world from the moment of colonization to the present day.[4] The second point is based on the assumption that political independence does not end colonialism because colonialism continues in a neocolonial mode in many societies. Postcolonialism is based on the "historical fact" of European colonialism and "diverse material effects" to which the phenomenon gave rise and thus for these authors is not the generic study of marginality.

How one defines "postcolonialism" is significant because that definition influences the potential duration of the "conditions" of "colony" and the degree to which these are marked merely by European imperialism.

8.1.1 Globalization and Wallerstein's World-System Model

The rapid globalization of culture in recent decades has revived an interest in relationships between economic centers of capital and peripheral economies. Analysis of empire and colonization has become fashionable in former colonizing nations, especially among intellectuals who have migrated from ex-colonized areas. Postcolonial studies fill a vacuum left by the collapse of some Marxist programs, yet the theoretical framework of postcolonialism is clearly indebted to Immanuel Wallerstein's Marxist-influenced theory of center–periphery world economic systems.

Wallerstein's 1974 book *The Modern World-System: Capitalist Agriculture and the Origins of the European World-Economy in the Sixteenth Century* offers a neo-Marxist account of economic development that was heavily influenced by the socioeconomic history of the French Annales.[5] He describes a deep structure, a world system, consisting of a social system larger than any juridically defined political unit. The basic linkage of this system was economic, so the entity was economic instead of political. This world economy consisted of an economic movement from periphery to center because of the monopolistic trade advantages of the center. The primitive means of economic domination allowed world economies, such as China, Persia, and Rome, to develop into empires.

Three factors necessary to the establishment of a specifically capitalist world economy are (1) an expansion of the geographical confines in question (European world), (2) the development of specific methods of labor control for diverse products and regions within the world economy, and (3) the evolution in core states of state machineries sufficiently strong to maintain control. The Western European core areas are thus examined in interplay with the semiperiphery and periphery. Beginning in the mid-fifteenth century, a capitalist world economy arose in Europe based on a worldwide division of labor: free labor at the core and forced labor at the periphery. Bureaucratic state machineries existed at the political core, but the system was not one of world empire under a single political system. This integrated world-economy system provided the structural basis for capitalism to maneuver because the economy could operate in areas larger than that controlled by the core's political entity.

Wallerstein does not argue that Europe was the only world economy in the sixteenth century but that it was the only world economy to proceed down a capitalist path. The slow rise of centralized states included the growth of systems of taxation and bureaucratic structures. Europe had a Christian civilization but neither a world empire nor a world economy until the "crisis of feudalism" brought new forms of taxation, or surplus appropriation, more conducive to a capitalist world economy. Wallerstein employs the terminology of the Annales to explain this feudal crisis as the conjuncture of secular trends, cyclical crisis, and climatological decline. The resulting appropriation of a surplus came to be based on more efficient and expanded productivity by means of a world market mechanism with the "artificial" assistance of state machineries, none of which controlled the world market in its entirety. The development of capitalism is thus understood to be the accumulation of corporate capital through an international division of labor.

Wallerstein has continued his analysis in three further volumes. The fourth volume ends with a brief outline of his plans for volumes five and six. His world-systems analysis has posed a range of methodological issues for historians. He moves the discussion beyond the art-versus-science debate, or the ideographic humanism–versus–nomothetic science debate as he refers to it, toward issues of how perceptions of reality correspond to the real world. His newest volume in the series, *Centrist Liberalism Triumphant* (2011), offers a critical history of the nineteenth-century creation of the social sciences (specifically the trinity of economics, sociology, and political science). He sees these as tools of centrist liberalism that have allowed dominant groups to control others.

Since the sixteenth century, the modern world system has been a capitalist world-economy. The triumph of centrist liberalism in the nineteenth century created a geoculture of values shared throughout the world system. The focus on a geoculture moves the historical analysis of world systems beyond purely material considerations.

Wallerstein's world-system theory postulates that capitalism since the sixteenth century has developed across national boundaries with an economic center influencing peripheral areas. The economic domination of emergent nations is thus understood as a world system that emphasizes the interconnections cutting across disparate situations. Historians who use this model to examine "local" knowledge are able to examine a specific, contingent culture and argue that the local issues are part of a global situation without being forced into specific notions of universal history. Local studies thus have a broader, and inherently comparative, context. Postcolonialists reject universal theorizing, but they seek broad comparative contexts for their local studies.

8.1.2 Orientalism

Despite the inherent comparative context of the center/semiperiphery/periphery model, critics claim that it restricts all studies to the analysis of a dominant group at the core with ethnic groups on the margins. This approach champions a form of Eurocentrism because all that happens can only be understood relative to the Eurocentric logic of accumulation. The representation of others to Europe becomes a projection of European fears and desires shrouded in a mask of local "objective" knowledge. Edward Said unmasked notions of Eurocentric universalism that are based on assumptions of European superiority in *Orientalism*, an examination of how Europeans define the East as the exotic "other" that is morally inferior to the West.[6]

Significant historical issues involving truth, morality, law, and polity are at stake in this social construction of a superior European self relative to an inferior Oriental. The representation of otherness is less an analysis of different peoples and societies and more a projection of European values. The East becomes a projection of vices that the West does not want to admit it possesses, such as cruelty, sensuality, laziness, and terror. The otherness of the East homogenizes inhabitants of the region into anonymous masses that act upon instinctive emotions instead of conscious individual decisions. These emotional reactions are thus given racial rationalizations that are not a product of individual rationalization. In other words, we see the world not as it is, but as we are.

Orientalism offered a subversive criticism of Western knowledge because it dispelled oppositional conventions, such as Orient versus

Occident, and destroyed Western colonial boundaries that persisted because of Western hegemony. Said sought to rediscover portions of native culture that have been, and continue to be, shaped by imperialism. He distinguished *imperialism*—the practice, theory, and attitudes of a dominating center ruling a distant territory—from *colonialism*. Colonialism is part of a broader process of capitalist imperialism whereby domination over another group is established and maintained because the other group is viewed as subordinate. Said posed a chronological ordering: "direct colonialism has largely ended," but "imperialism . . . lingers where it has always been, in a kind of general cultural sphere as well as in specific political, ideological, economic, and social practices."[7]

Heightened sensitivity to the culture of imperialism is part of the postcolonial perspective. Postcolonial studies are written about, as well as from, the margins and thus seek to unsettle this imperialism by restructuring and reinscribing authority. The construction of an "imagined community" from which to invent a new self-image is one mechanism for countering imperialist oppression. But this raises problems related to nationalism and the creation of national myths. Frantz Fanon, for instance, warns against national consciousness because the local bourgeoisie use this nationalism for their own ends.

Said's own solution is to be found in humanist scholarship that supersedes Eurocentric stereotypes and universals. Humanism somehow rises above local political and cultural conditions. Critics have attacked his reliance on humanist ideals, such as individual genius, as a convenient avenue for undermining Eurocentric essentialisms but as an insufficient means to explain change.

8.1.3 White Mythologies

Robert Young moved the discussion beyond orientalism in his 1990 book *White Mythologies: Writing History and the West.* He claimed that Said's Orientalism "operates both as a poison and cure for Europe: it constitutes both the greatest threat to European civilization at the same time as it represents a therapeutic for the lost spiritual values of the West, offering hope for the regeneration of Europe by Asia."[8] Orientalism offers a position partially outside of European scholarship but not far enough outside for Young. He called for a reformulated grand theory that is not tainted by what he considers the colonialist, racist tradition of European historicism.

Young traces the ideas of several individual theorists in an attempt to delineate how colonialism and racism haunt the writing of history. Marx's confidence in progress allowed him to explain all societies with a single theory of development. The Western writing of history defined all non-Europeans as people without a history who are folded into the history of the West. Such a writing of history is a Western imposition. Young considers how we might write a history of non-Europeans that is more than a simple footnote added to European history.

> In addition to the rewriting of the history of non-European histories and cultures, analysis of colonialism therefore shifts the perspective of European history and culture so as to interrogate the fundamental structures and assumptions of Western knowledge. The legacy of colonialism is as much a problem for the West as it is for the scarred lands in the world beyond.[9]

In the final two chapters, Young turns to the works of Homi Bhabha and Gayatri Chakravorty Spivak to show the extent to which history, specifically Eurocentric historicism, is racist and colonial. Young's analysis forced historians to reconsider how they might write about non-Europeans with theories and categories that are not tainted by European assumptions and traditions. His solution to this problematic enterprise is the deconstruction of the primacy of the European "West." A decade later, Young began to champion the notion of tricontintentalism as a solution. His strong position differs from that of Spivak who seems more tentative and provisional about this. Young's *White Mythologies* had a profound influence on scholars floating between history and literary theory who were looking for alternatives to the neo-historicists. This, and the fact that he turned to Bhabha and Spivak, gave momentum to the bourgeoning field of postcolonial studies.

8.2 THE LANGUAGE OF SELF/OTHER AND IN-BETWEEN SPACES

The analysis of conceptual boundaries, such as Said's Oriental versus Occidental and Wallerstein's core versus periphery, was a standard component of early postcolonial critics. The binary analysis of inside versus outside, as well as self versus other, has since been replaced by nonbinary tropes that emphasize the space existing between the binary oppositions. Tropes such as hybridity, diaspora, migration, creolization, and transculturation provide an avenue to understand the binary extremes by analyzing the blurred spaces, languages, and identities that occur when people move between spaces. Migrants occupy multiple spaces and combine languages in a manner similar to the global crisscrossing of abstract forces. By exploring the ideas and languages of those who move between definable spaces, postcolonialists are able to analyze power relations and boundaries from a new perspective.

8.2.1 Hybridity

Homi Bhabha's analysis of hybridity as the unstable double identity of people crossing cultures is consistent with postmodernism's analysis of fields of discourse evident in Derrida's textuality and Foucault's emphasis on the construction of identity. Hybridity emphasizes the mutual development of new traditions that combine the colonizer and the colonized. This two-way transaction, as opposed to the one-way notion that colonizers simply silence the colonized, recognizes that aspects of the oppressed culture are formed into the new culture. The mutuality of hybridity allows theorists a way to escape binary conceptualizations and avoid monolithic models of cultural exchange. The profound instability of the double identity, neither of the one world nor the other, is evident in the way that language is permanently tainted by the interaction between colonizer and colonized.

Said stresses the way that texts are instruments of control, whereas Bhabha's focus on hybridity shows ways in which texts can reveal the "necessary deformation and displacement of all sites of discrimination and domination."[10] The hybrid texts are thus interesting because they contain elements of both the oppressor and the oppressed. One fertile avenue of study is the extent to which hybrid texts are the voice of the oppressor and the extent to which they are the voice of the oppressed. Whenever the oppressed use the language of an oppressor, they employ mimicry. Mimetic modes of expression are especially evident in colonies where the colonized mimes the master with a partial, and intentionally distorted, representation. This representation threatens the colonizer and offers an alternative to Said's notion of the colonized "possessed entirely" by the colonizer.

8.2.2 Subaltern Studies and Postmodernism

Hybrid texts by definition include traces of the colonized and the colonizer. One radical branch within postcolonialism focuses on voices that have not been tainted by the colonizer. This branch looks to earlier works by Frantz Fanon as a model for rejecting the European-tainted tradition of the hybrid and seeks instead to find the "subaltern" voices. The "subaltern" is "the *ideal* figure of the person who survives actively, even joyously, on the assumption that the statist instruments of domination will always belong to somebody else and never aspires to them."[11] The "subaltern" opposes colonial dominance without participating in academic discourse that is itself a form of the European universalism that is supposedly being rejected.

The rejection of universality, the interest in mimicry, and the pursuit of hybrid and "subaltern" texts are based on postmodern assumptions that language structures the way an individual encounters the world. Language itself can be imperialistic because it is based on certain historical assumptions about the world. For instance, the way that a language is employed to name, and thus understand or know, something reveals the values underlying that language. Postcolonial theory is full of postmodern methods and writings that, for all their efforts to debunk European logocentrism, are products of the European core and thus are the colonizer's language of naming the colonized.

Despite its strong European taint, postmodernism does offer a healthy suspicion about the objectivity of historical consciousness and thereby provides an intellectual attitude that postcolonialists find attractive. And while postmodernism offered no Archimedean point for establishing moral judgments, postcolonialists are eager to produce oppositional truth claims that provide avenues for judgment and action.

Whereas postmodernism's focus on the text instead of the referent rendered it powerless for directing change, postcolonialism's reading of texts demands the establishment of a colonized referent in order to resist the colonists. Postcolonialism thus flourishes in the postmodern intellectual setting because it remains consistent with postmodern skepticism yet it also offers an opportunity for postulating political and social programs that could not be championed by postmodernists. Namely, postcolonialism encourages the championing of truths that are oppositional. A prerequisite for postcolonial political engagement involves what Gayatri Spivak calls "unlearning privilege." Postcolonialists utilize the postmodern suspension of the referent when reading texts of the colonialists, but they create new referents that will challenge oppression.

Some have argued that postcolonialism's current prestige within academia derives from its closeness to postmodernism. Both decenter discourse and employ such subversive strategies as mimicry, parody, and irony. But one deconstructs European master narratives, and the other offers a discourse of oppositionality that seeks to influence postcolonial cultures. This association with colonialism, much like feminism's association with patriarchy, provides a political agenda that is not evident in postmodernism.

Most postcolonialists actively work toward social change by conjuring up political issues in their intellectual pursuit. One self-proclaimed postcolonialist claims that to be a postcolonialist is to be a *card-carrying postcolonial discontent*. The real issue becomes *antioppression*, be it in the colonial or postcolonial society as well as in academia. Dipesh Chakrabarty goes so far as to claim that the postcolonial writing of "subaltern history, that is, documenting resistance to oppression and exploitation, must be part of a larger effort to make the world more socially just."[12] This attention to oppression, even oppression within institutions of higher education, forces historians to reconsider how cultures privilege knowledge. The ramifications for history are significant because this challenges historians to reconsider whether hybrid, migratory, minority, or underprivileged groups are best studied within existing paradigms or whether new conceptualizations need to be created. At this level, postcolonialism no longer takes European models and adapts them to postcolonial subject matter. Instead, postcolonialism constructs new categories that are distinct from European norms. If history involves the otherness of the past, then postcolonialism questions who the "we" of the present are and what our history legitimates. This questioning of ourselves combined with the focus on hybridity and mimicry encourages us to contemplate other ways of conceptualizing that otherness. Whether these new conceptualizations will "make the world more socially just" remains to be seen.

8.3 POSTCOLONIALISM AND THE CRISIS OF HISTORICAL REPRESENTATION

Where there is community, there is also exclusion, for boundaries are crucial. Categories, be they universal or local, colonial or postcolonial, result in the rejections of certain memories. These rejections are not inherently bad, but the unintended consequences of those rejections may prove problematic. For instance, Romanticism and Pietism both rejected the rationality of the European Enlightenment. Initially Romanticism harmed no one and showed little potential for violence. Pietism on the other hand was deemed dangerous by many "intellectuals" who disliked its insistence upon devout religious experiences. The long-term repercussions of the two movements have been quite disparate. It is difficult to find connections between Pietism and violence, whereas Romanticism can be linked directly to nineteenth-century nationalism and twentieth-century fascism. Romanticism as a movement was neither violent nor oppressive, but some Romantic works contributed unexpectedly to movements that were violent and oppressive. In terms of violence, Pietism was more effective than Romanticism in making the "world more socially just." Both postmodernism and postcolonialism reject the developmental optimism of post-Enlightenment European theorists. The language of postmodernism has successfully captured the attention of academics around the world. Whether postcolonialists will come to share the same success has much to do with the historical representations that they create.

What sort of voice will postcolonialists have now that they are located within the academy? Are postcolonialists forced to prove that they are not politically indifferent because, as part of the academy, they are not different? Some critics claim that postcolonialists fail to confront exploitation directly and thus allow students to "feel good" about discussing exploitation. These discussions provide students a safe experience with diversity through managed encounters. The margins remain manageable when they are defined by the center. Intellectuals outside of the core areas are not primarily preoccupied with their contact with Europe. But postcolonialism generalizes a variety of histories and then links them to the European core either directly or as counterexamples. Causal change is always produced by, for, or against the European core; hence, otherness as a concept remains haunted by the logic of Western historicism.

Furthermore, the paradigm of rational actors dominates most postcolonial studies. Homi Bhabha and Veena Das have questioned paradigms of social action defined by rational actors, but thus far postcolonialists have yet to offer an alternative to the paradigm of rational actors. Is it possible to reject all universalizing theories but to base all analysis upon a notion of universal rationality?

Despite the taint of the European core, postcolonialism offers an awareness of otherness in a comparative model that greatly exceeds the Eurocentrism of most Western history. It offers a method for evaluating dialogues of similarity and difference without being trapped in the binary model of oppressor and oppressed. The existence of hybridized oppositions and boundaries allows postcolonialists to examine the cultural relationships of power. Analysis of these power relations can include analysis of the wide-ranging implications of policy and thus of historical interpretations that inform policy. The increased attention to power and language provides fascinating opportunities for cultural historians.

Postcolonialism frees historians of Europe from European models of history and encourages historians to contemplate other methods of framing knowledge. For instance, Steven Feierman argues in "Africa in History: The End of Universal Narratives" that

> the problem here is that categories of historical analysis, even though ostensibly value-neutral, are drawn from Europe, and therefore the historian looks in Africa for a familiar constellation of kings, nobles, church and merchants. . . . If what is European is defined as normal, then the non-European appears to be disordered, abnormal, primitive. The categories that are ostensibly universal are in fact particular, and they refer to the experience of modern Europe.[13]

Postcolonialism's ramifications for historians of noncolonized areas are significant because of the "crisis of historical representation that came about when historians began to hear the voices of those who had been voiceless, and the more general epistemological crisis affecting all the social sciences and humanities."[14] Feierman's "crisis" does not mean an end to European history, but rather an awareness of otherness outside of Europe. Foucault's analysis of the other within European society, such as in his study of madness, had a profound influence on the writing of history, yet historians who were quick to embrace Foucault have been slow to acknowledge postcolonialism's analysis of the "other" outside of Europe.

8.4   THE PROVINCIALIZATION OF EUROPE?

Perhaps one reason for postcolonialism's slow inroads into Western academia has been its strong focus on theory instead of historical analysis. Microhistorians wrote microhistories and then turned to a discussion of the craft of writing microhistory whereas postcolonialists and "Big History" macrohistorians have tended to take the opposite approach, namely they discuss theory before actually writing postcolonial or macrohistorical histories. Combine the paucity of postcolonial histories relative to works on postcolonial theory with the mute nature of actual subalterns and the writing of true postcolonial history becomes difficult.

The best exemplars of postcolonialism have tended to be collections of essays that combine subject-specific analysis with general theorizing. Currently, the most widely discussed postcolonial book is Dipesh Chakrabarty's *Provincializing Europe: Postcolonial Thought and Historical Difference*. The subtitle reveals the postcolonial debt to Derrida and other postmodernists. The title also reveals the extent to which postcolonialism represents a rejection of European intellectual hegemony. Or perhaps, it is better to say, an attempt to reject the role of the European intellectual tradition; Chakrabarty is clearly indebted to Marx and Heidegger. Surprisingly, the concluding chapter grounds the book in the very European intellectual history that is being provincialized: "provincializing Europe cannot ever be a project of shunning European thought. For at the end of European imperialism, European thought is a gift to us all."[15]

Is provincializing Europe new or even necessary? European grand theory may not be the best way to explain the history of India, but was it ever the best way to explain the history of Europe? Eugene J. Weber showed in his 1976 book *From Peasants into Frenchmen: The Modernization of Rural France 1870–1914* that "European" was not a category adequate to describe nineteenth-century French peasants.[16] Have postcolonialists offered better means of theorizing or simply added a nail to the coffin of Grand Theorizing?

Furthermore, could "provincializing Europe" in favor of postcolonial categories simply become another form of Orientalism (taken in the negative context that Said meant whereby it projects what the postcolonialists do not want to be rather than describing what actually exists)? The current fashion of placing postcolonial discussions in opposition to the evil European "other" assumes both homogeneity in Europe and that non-European voices offer better models for understanding humanity. To some critics, postcolonialism would seem to fall short if it is nothing more than a pendulum swinging the other direction.

This is not to suggest that all history is the history of oppression. Some would argue that Pietism has proven to be a better rejection of Enlightenment oppression than has Romanticism. But, as Chakrabarty shows, all Romanticism need not be dismissed simply because "romanticism now reminds them (leftist intellectuals in the West) only of the Nazis. It would be sad if we ceded this entire heritage (romantic nationalism in India) to the Hindu extremists out of a fear that our romanticism must be the same as whatever the European placed under that name in their histories."[17] Such a fear would be "a greater instance of submission to a Eurocentric imagination."

Chakrabarty and other postcolonialists want to decenter Europe, but if that decentering prohibits other voices from being heard, that would seem to defeat the purpose. Perhaps the academic endorsement that postcolonialism has come to enjoy will actually undermine its goal of giving voice to the oppressed. No longer a movement of transnational intellectuals, postcolonialism is now fully ensconced in mainstream academia around the world. Postcolonial theory has offered invigorating criticism of European thought in general, but the actual writing of postcolonial history is still in its infancy. It remains to be seen whether postcolonial history will offer more than Italian Microhistory, German Alltagsgeschichte, and British Marxist social history.

When the dust settles, part of postcolonialism's legacy will be its influence on the writing of history. The nineteenth-century pursuit of scientific history marginalized claims of moral or political historical interpretation. Postcolonialism offers an alternative to scientific history and to the single narrative truth that Ranke sought in his representation of events as they actually happened. Freed of that objectivity and those narrative truths, postcolonial history fosters new ways of configuring the past that are inherently moral and political. Postcolonial history is forcing a healthy reassessment of the writing of history, the scope of historical pursuit, and the moral implications of historically constructed communal memories.

But where there is community there is also exclusion, for boundaries are crucial. It remains to be seen whether the postcolonial communal memory will fulfill Chakrabarty's goal and "make the world more socially just."

NOTES

1.   J. Jorge Klor de Alva, "The Postcolonization of the (Latin) American Experience: A Reconsideration of 'Colonialism,' 'Postcolonialism,' and 'Mestizaje,'" in Gyan Prakash (ed.), *After Colonialism: Imperial Histories and Postcolonial Displacements* (Princeton, NJ: Princeton University Press, 1995), pp. 241–275, here p. 245.

2.   Homi K. Bhabha, "In a Spirit of Calm Violence," in Gyan Prakash (ed.), *After Colonialism: Imperial Histories and Postcolonial Displacements* (Princeton, NJ: Princeton University Press, 1995), pp. 326–343, here pp. 326–327.

3.   Bill Ashcroft, Gareth Griffiths, and Helen Tiffin, *The Empire Writes Back: Theory and Practice in Post-Colonial Literatures* (New York: Routledge, 1989), p. 2.

4.   Bill Ashcroft, Gareth Griffiths, and Helen Tiffin, *The Post-Colonial Studies Reader* (New York: Routledge, 1995), p. xv.

5.   Immanuel Wallerstein, *The Modern World-System: Capitalist Agriculture and the Origins of the European World-Economy in the Sixteenth Century* (New York: Academic Press, 1974).

6.   Edward Said, *Orientalism* (New York: Pantheon, 1978).

7.   Edward Said, *Culture and Imperialism* (New York: Random House, 1993), p. 9.

8.   Robert Young, *White Mythologies: Writing History and the West* (New York: Routledge, 1990), p. 140.

9.   Ibid., p. 126.

10.   Ashcroft et al., *The Post-Colonial Studies Reader*, p. 9.

11.   Dipesh Chakrabarty, *Habitations of Modernity: Essays in the Wake of Subaltern Studies* (Chicago: University of Chicago Press, 2002), p. 36.

12.   Dipesh Chakrabarty, *Provincializing Europe: Postcolonial Thought and Historical Difference* (Princeton, NJ: Princeton University Press, 2000), p. 117.

13.   Steven Feierman, "Africa in History: The End of Universal Narratives," in Gyan Prakash (ed.), *After Colonialism: Imperial Histories and Postcolonial Displacements* (Princeton, NJ: Princeton University Press, 1995), pp. 40–65, here pp. 48–50.

14.   Ibid., p. 51.

15.   Chakrabarty, *Provincializing Europe*, p. 255.

16.   Eugen J. Weber, *From Peasants into Frenchmen: The Modernization of Rural France 1870–1914* (Stanford, CA: Stanford University Press, 1976).

17.   Chakrabarty, *Habitations of Modernity*, p. 37.

Chapter 9

New Terminology and Progress

It is time for the last chapter in the roommate saga. It is time for you to begin living a life that is truly post-roommate. You are now free to discard all remnants of the previous roommate. In fact, you have come to realize that you really could not care less about the missing roommate. Nevertheless, the process of creating a historical account of the roommate has proved to be most fruitful because it has allowed you to understand better just what type of person you would like to be.

Your own history of the missing roommate has created a meaningful memory that could prove useful to you. This memory could be useful not because another roommate will disappear but rather because you will now be better equipped to deal with a range of social interactions. Both your identity and your conception of the type of person you would like to be are products of your past and the memory of that past. Memory is essential for evaluating your personal identity. In fact, freeing yourself of the roommate may free you to re-member, or reconstruct, who you are.

This need not be an individual process. Various communal memories create new communities, be they nations, ethnic groups, neighbors, or others. The commonality of any community is most easily delineated by analysis of its fringes because a community's borders are defined by its treatment of the hybrid, marginal, and alien. Marginality should not be pursued in and of itself because such a pursuit would fail to reflect on the community as a whole. Historians who are aware of postcolonialism's notions of the hybrid and the marginal may find avenues for germinating new approaches to history.

There is much to be said for the contemporary process of innovation, renewal, and fermentation in the historical profession without appeal to some lost "golden age" from which history has fallen. The cry of "crisis" is inappropriate today because history is less doctrinaire and exclusionary than ever before. The contemporary historiographical vitality exists precisely because innovative historians are challenging the borders of the historical community. The ensuing reconstruction of history is fruitful because recent self-scrutiny has made historians more conscious of the conceptual underpinnings of history just as the self-scrutiny you underwent during the roommate episode has made you more conscious of your assumptions, modes of self-expression, and avenues of self-representation.

The newest forms of historical analysis are evidence of historical vitality, but they may also render the past less complicated. Efforts to make the past rational and logical have also produced new terminology and theories that might surprise historical actors from the past. For instance, "modernism" has been redefined such that famous modernists, like the British "modernist" novelists of the early twentieth century, would not recognize themselves as modernists. The rise of postmodernism included with it a redefinition of "modernism" because postmodern thinkers see themselves as post-modern. Postmodernists by definition reject modernism and thus postmodernism has fueled a heated debate about modernism, modernization, modernity, and progress in general. New definitions allow historians to be more precise in addressing the past, but they also force other historians to view the past through presentist lenses.

The very existence of postcolonial studies as a subfield within history superimposes a presentist terminology on an era. The shift from colonial to postcolonial happened at different times, paces, and avenues across the globe. The term itself imposes a unitary timeline of precolonial, colonial, and postcolonial onto something that was experienced quite differently contingent on time and place. This does not mean that the term "postcolonial" should not be used, but that historians should recognize that the term simplifies a complicated past and creates an understanding of the past that might itself be foreign to those who lived through it. Robert Young attempts to liberate postcolonialism from euro-based terminology by utilizing the term "tricontinentalism." The Eurocentric definition of the movement as something coming out of the colonialists' world (postcolonial) is thus rejected and the movement comes to be defined positively from the perspective of inhabitants of the three continents of Africa, Asia, and Latin America. This employment of new terminology creates a contemporary understanding that allows us to grasp the past in ways that the participants themselves would view as strange. It also pinpoints neat and clean origins to movements that were complicated and messy. Both the use of present-day labels to clarify the past and attempts to pinpoint precise origins for complicated things are dangers inherent in the writing of history. One needs to render the past meaningful and abridged, but one does not want to change the past in so doing.

Postmodernism and postcolonialism have forced a radical rethinking of the scope of historical study. The master narratives of Western discourse are no longer applicable in all places at all times. The grand old narratives appear overdetermined in a world that looks underdetermined. Political states have traditionally crafted histories, or perhaps myths, of origins. These histories of national origin are less apt to be challenged in powerful states than in weak states. All histories of national origin are susceptible to criticism from historians of world history, but the growth of courses on world civilizations does not mean that nation-states cannot craft histories of themselves. The fields of World Civilizations and global studies do require the use of new categories and methods and thus even national histories will be recreated to fit the era of global history. Historians who seek a wider audience will need to acknowledge the historical contingency of their own accounts and the wide diversity of other accounts.

9.1   TRICONTINENTALISM

Immanuel Wallerstein's model of core and periphery (Chapter 8) suggests that there is a core, or central driving world, around which the periphery revolves. The term "Third World" was used frequently in the late twentieth century to define a backward world that was below the first and second worlds. "Third World" as a term has long been controversial among Marxist theorists because the first world was a Western world of economic domination with the second world being the Marxist states and the Third World consisting of everything else. Robert Young champions the term "tricontinentalism" as an alternative to Third World and even postcolonialism. The term comes from a 1966 conference in Havana, Cuba, of the Organization of Solidarity of the Peoples of Africa, Asia, and Latin America. The three continents of Africa, Asia, and Latin America constitute a tricontinental that Young identifies with the Havana Tricontinental of 1966. He sees this as the initial global alliance of peoples from those three continents against imperialism. He also believes that the Havana Tricontinental and its journal *Tricontinental* are the origins of modern postcolonial theory. Young goes so far as to suggest that the term "tricontinentalism" would be a better option than "postcolonialism."

Tricontinental critique is built on the presupposition that European expansion from Christopher Columbus until the end of World War II differed from other forms of oppression in terms of depth, scope, and legacy.

European colonialization was a deeply entrenched worldwide movement that forced diverse peoples to give up their local identities, join in new societies as defined by outsiders, and follow down the Western path of economic development. Justifications for European expansion were frequently based on moral grounds, yet the cost of this expansion involved unprecedented human suffering. The pursuit of economic domination created cultural suffering. Tricontinental theory moves beyond European Marxism, with its focus on material analysis, and turns to analysis of culture in order to delineate the underlying forces of oppression and coercive domination. Tricontinentalism calls for a new theory to deal with the horrors of the colonial experience.

The relationship between theory and history has long been debated. Chakrabarty's project of provincializing Europe floundered when he, despite his eagerness to engage non-European terminology, failed to move beyond Hegel and Marx. Hegelian-Marxism has been sufficiently tainted by Eurocentricism that some scholars refer to it as "Western Marxism." Robert Young's championing of the term "tricolonialism" is an attempt to free theory from the Eurocentric taint of Western Marxism by saving aspects of materialism without the full baggage of Hegelian-Marxism.

Young's project is part of a broader recognition that metaphors are useful to facilitate dialogue because one does not need to redefine a position when one can simply offer the name of a theorist as an abbreviated way of presenting the entire theory. Metaphors facilitate communication, but as metaphors wear over time, they tend to destabilize the effectiveness of communication. The baggage of Eurocentric thinkers has forced a retooling of the entire use of theory, metaphors, and categories.

Young claims that Foucault failed to resolve differences between his "historical materialist and institutional account of discursive events . . . and other available materialist positions, particularly Marxism."[1] He believes that the "theoretical kernel of postcolonial theory itself" (based on the works of Bhabha and Spivak) allows scholars to move toward a tricontinentalism found in the "unresolved tension between colonialism as an institutional performative discourse of power-knowledge and colonialism according to the dialectical formations elaborated in tricontinental Marxism."[2] Foucault, Deleuze, and other European thinkers moved to a non-Marxist historical materialism that is not as vibrant as tricontinental Marxism. Young's tricontinental postcolonialists carry the day by casting aside Euroecentric theorists but maintaining awareness of Marx's materialism.

The history of non-Europeans ceases to be a process of explaining other peoples as simple footnotes to European history. Non-Europeans are no longer lacking their own histories. They are no longer treated as a unitary group that is either woven into the history of the West or condemned relative to Western standards of progress. Western notions of rationality and knowledge cease to be the standard to which all other cultures are compared. The modernist and the European Enlightenment projects of rationalizing the world and comparing everything to the "maturity" of Europe cease to be acceptable. Europe is no longer the implicit master narrative to which all others are compared. Instead, tricontinentalism posits the possibility of alternative systems of knowledge: world views of the dispossessed and the subaltern are taken seriously.

Both "postcolonialism" and "tricontinentalism" are terms that pinpoint precise origins to a movement that is complicated and messy. Despite Young's ambitious efforts, the term "tricontinentalism" has not replaced "postcolonialism" as the term that scholars use to explain the pursuit of the world views of the dispossessed and the subaltern. Some scholars question whether the perspectives of the dispossessed and subaltern are too broad to be translated into simplistic labels. Malini Johar Schueller takes exception to postcolonialists' pursuit of neutral terms such as "global." She fears that the rejection of politically charged terms, like "racism" and "imperialism," are "global" but still reveal the underlying structural inequalities.[3] She is concerned that the newest universalizing theory of postcolonialists fails to capture the unique racial oppressions that some racialized groups have experienced. The postmodern celebration of all minority identities as similar in their resistance undermines individual groups. Schueller offers one of the few voices within the contemporary postcolonial discourse that is critical of the evolving vocabulary of universal theory. She calls for postcolonialists to craft alternative narratives that reveal the legacies of specific histories, regardless of how unpleasant those histories may be. Official memory, national histories, and universalist theories may not encompass the brutal past that continues to structure the lives of many people.

9.2 THE ECLIPSE OF MODERNISM: MODERNISM(S), MODERNIZATION(S), AND MODERNITY(IES)

> The "past" which modernists think ratifies the present, and the "past" from which postmodernists think they can so easily emancipate themselves, is a "past" which they first select in order to prove their point. So we draw a veil over happier possibilities as well as over darker ones; our need to reconcile ourselves with the worlds in which we live forbids us to raise that veil and take seriously the world we have lost.[4]

The rise of postmodernism has forced a radical retooling of the term "modernism" and the related terms "modernization" and "modernity." The Enlightenment project to rationalize the world had its origins in the scientific theories that moved the basic understanding of the world from a qualitative science (things are defined based on their qualities) to quantitative science. Alfred Crosby argued in *The Measure of Reality: Quantification and Western Society, 1250–1600* that a new model that was visual and quantitative came to offer Europeans a new way to examine reality. The shift to quantitative perceptions of reality and the rise of the new science's geocentric (earth-centered) universe meant that motion was universal and thus Europeans could reason and explain things that were previously mysterious. Enlightenment modernism built upon Western ideas of measurement, rationality, knowledge, and development as a universal standard. All other cultures could be evaluated by the extent to which they embraced Western rationality, knowledge, and progress.

Modernist notions of history were based on the presupposition that things unfolded along the most probable course. The logical unfolding of the most rational course of events resulted in narratives that were neat and tidy, but that overdetermined causation. Some scholars sought to redefine "modernism" according to the Enlightenment tradition of unfolding rational truth. They tended to offer objective and encyclopedic coverage of modernism such as Peter Gay's book *Modernism: The Lure of Heresy* (2007). Postmodernists tend to break from this teleological narrative and thus they call for a new understanding of modernism. Gabriel Josipovici's *What Ever Happened to Modernism?* (2010) is an attempt to capture the spirit of modernism from the postmodern perspective. Josipovici offered a short account wherein he acknowledges the difficulty of the task while pursuing the spirit of modernism more than some comprehensive definition of "modernism":

> Naturally I think the story I have just finished telling is the true one. At the same time I recognize that there are many stories and there is no such thing as *the* true story, only more or less plausible explanations, stories that take more or less account of the facts. I am aware too that these stories are *sites of contestation*; more is at stake than how we view the past. That is what is wrong with positivist accounts of Modernism, which purport simply to "tell the story" . . . These make a show at impartiality but are of course just as partial as any other account.[5]

For Josipovici there is not a "definitive 'story' of Modernism. We cannot step outside of it, much as we would like to, and pronounce with authority on it. We can only try to persuade people to see it from our point of view."[6] And we all have a point of view just as each modernist— Josipovici focuses mainly on literary figures in his book—reconfigured modernism.

Modernism in its most limited meaning defines an early twentieth-century movement of European creative arts that broke with the realism and linear narrative of the nineteenth century. Virginia Woolf's novel *Mrs. Dalloway* is a story of one character preparing for and giving a party, but the story is told by a stream-of-consciousness account from the perspective of diverse characters. The reader is thrust into the mind of one character and then another, only to realize that the past is haunting the present in ways that are unseen and unknown to the other characters. The past can haunt us because there is a darker side of humanity evident for instance in Joseph Conrad's *Heart of Darkness*. It is only possible to be modern relative to someone who is not and thus modernism involved moving beyond the past. Josipovici concludes his book with a rhetorical question: "In other words, are we to see our own history, that which makes us what we are, as something which blinkers us or which sharpens our visions? This is, in itself, of course, a very Modernist question."[7] The essence of modernism is the dilemma of whether or not one has improved and become better than another. Difference is not enough; improvement is the issue. To be modern contains an implicit comparison because someone is only modern relative to someone who is not modern.

Dipesh Chakrabarty concluded a roundtable essay aptly entitled "The Muddle of Modernity" in the *American Historical Review* with a reminder of the ideological nature of defining modernity:

> To be "modern" is to judge one's experience of time and space and thus create new possibilities for oneself. But it is also to take intellectual and political risks, for the very act of judging opens us up to the criticism of others, including the criticism of those to come . . . Historians have to take responsibility for the normative freight that the word "modernity," with all its diverse and somewhat slippery meanings, has carried globally since the time of European colonialism.[8]

Terms change meanings over time as scholars pursue new ways to explain the past. Questioning the meaning(s) of modernity led to questions about paths to modernization(s) and possible modernity(ies). Historians after Joan Kelly questioned the commonly accepted periodization of history and thus began using terms like "early-modern" to define what had previously been known as Renaissance and Reformation Europe. Kelly astutely questioned whether women had in fact experienced a Renaissance, but the ensuing switch to early-modern Europe contained its own modernist championing of Western triumphalism. Comparative sociology and history often sought to put the world within a chronological measure of progress based on Western notions. Comparative History is far from dead, but most comparative historians now avoid language that would suggest a teleological unfolding of progress—a theory of modernization.

European and American historians of the late nineteenth century followed Leopold von Ranke's tradition of primary source analysis of nation-states. The unifications of Italy and of Germany into distinct nations, as well the reunification of the United States after its Civil War, were cultural factors that encouraged national histories. In the early twentieth century, some Western historians shifted the focus to something larger than the nation-state. They did not deny the significance of nation-states, but they sought cultural and cross-cultural categories that were better suited for global analysis. This widening of focus still used ancient Greek and Roman cultures as models and thus remained trapped in Western categories and concepts. By mid-century, theorists in a number of the social sciences turned to functionalist arguments to explain modernization as a process. Shortly after World War II, Walt Whitman Rostow (W. W. Rostow) developed a five-stage model of development and economic modernization that became a foundation for the field of modernization theory. The economic underpinnings of the purported progress of modernization became a staple component of sociologists and economists.

Modernization theory had a teleological unfolding of development whereby all societies progressed. The model assumes that others will develop along the same pattern as Western societies. European modernity became a standard to which the rest of the world fell woefully behind. The ethnocentric bias of the theory is evident, but the ideas were used to inform policy decisions in regard to colonies and countries breaking free from colonization. Other countries were encouraged to follow the process of modernization and to become modern like Europe. Richard Wolin critiqued that "the risks of transposing Western notions of historicity or development to non-Western societies that possess less rigid and more flexible ideals of temporality are numerous. Such transpositions represent a form of cultural colonization."[9]

Criticism of developmental modernization theory arose among theorists of diverse political and ideological traditions, but none rejected the notion that differences existed and that some societies had technological innovations that were not available everywhere. The debate shifted from modernization to modernizations. Things were different but development need not follow one pattern and outcomes were unclear. Schmuel Eisenstadt was one of the Cold War modernization theorists who changed his theory in the 1990s to embrace the notion of multiple modernities. He separated modernity from modernization theory and suggested that cultural modernities were possible. Europe may have become modern first, but Eurocentric modernity was not the only cultural model for modernity.

Just as modernisms had replaced a single notion of modernism and modernizations had replaced modernization, it became problematic to embrace a singular notion of modernity. The use of the plural "modernities" suggests a wide range of potential outcomes, but at some point, the concept ceases to have meaning as an analytical tool. Richard Wolin is weary of professional historians crafting rarified definitions that have little meaning to outsiders. He concludes that we ultimately need some measure of self-meaning:

> Historians have justifiably rebelled against the Eurocentric normative consensus, which was so closely tied to the resumptions of modernization theory, but no clear replacement paradigm has yet emerged. At one point the historians' guild rejected political history—history "from above"—and embraced social history thereby seeking to lend a voice to those who were traditionally denied one. But here, too, they have been disappointed, insofar as the "wretched of the earth" often failed to live up to the progressive standards that Western intellectuals established from them. Some historians have turned to microhistory, unearthing vast stores of detail about the minutiae of historical life—to what end, however? Aesthetic approaches to history—a disinterested study of the past for its own sake—avoid the pitfalls of mainstream developmental approaches, but ultimately the end result seems scattershot, hit-or-miss.[10]

The shift from modernism, modernization, and modernity to modernisms, modernizations, and modernities, respectively, was all done from the best of intentions, but it reopened the issue of progress in the field of history: both progress in the sense of the profession making better sense of the past and progress in the sense of societal directionality and improvement. Modernist notions of history were based on the presupposition that things unfolded along the most probable course. This logical unfolding of the most rational course of events resulted in narratives that were neat and tidy, but that overly determined causation. The eclipse of modernist assumptions that events followed the most probable cause meant that grand narratives of modernization were too simplistic and deterministic for a world that looks underdetermined. The constantly changing categories that we use to explain historical causation suggest that perhaps the field of history is different but not better. The inherent teleology of modernism forces historians interested in change over time to rethink the entire notion of progress in the history.

9.3 PROGRESS IN HISTORY?

The question of progress in history is actually several questions of progress in history: (1) has the human condition improved, (2) are humans heading on a trajectory of improvement, and (3) do new methodologies and technologies allow for progress in the writing of history? The first two points were touched upon briefly in the previous pages, but they are complicated with much disagreement among historians. World population is growing and technology is changing, but does directionality equal improvement? Have opportunities for individuals and societies expanded or contracted? Historians are greatly divided on these issues, yet they continue to write history. And historians continue to employ new technologies and new methodologies in their pursuit of history. Does their participation in this adventure suggest that something positive, some progress, exists in the writing of history?

The notion of progress in history has been unpopular since Herbert Butterfield wrote *The Whig Interpretation of History* in 1931 to explain a school of nineteenth century historians (see Chapter 1). It is worth noting that most of the Whig historians were long dead before this label was used to describe them. The term "Whig history" has taken on a new meaning as a pejorative attack on any teleological history or history of progress. The continued use of the term suggests that it is a beneficial way to describe the past: historians are able to explain the past better than they were before Butterfield gave us this tool. The use of the term "Whig history" to condemn historians who believe in historical progress serves ironically to prove progress in the writing of history.

The academic discipline of history is more complicated than ever before. Subfields have flourished, terminology has expanded, and historical methodology has expanded, but complexity is not the same as progress. The current historical fashions push in opposite directions; microhistory narrows the focus and global history expands the focus, while the pool of historical remnants continuously expands. Despite the developments in theory and methodology, historians still aspire to craft perspectives that might enlighten our understanding of the past and the present. As Gabrielle Spiegel, then president of the American Historical Association, concluded her Presidential Address "The Task of the Historian" (2009): "In the last analysis, what is the past but a once material existence now silenced, extant only as sign and as sign drawing to itself chains of conflicting interpretations that hover over its absent presence and compete for possession of the relics, seeking to invest traces of significance upon the bodies of the dead."[11]

NOTES

1.   Robert J. C. Young, *Postcolonialism: An Historical Introduction* (Malden, MA: Blackwell Publishing, 2001), p. 410.

2.   Ibid., p. 410.

3.   Malini Johar Schueller, *Locating Race: Global Sites of Post-Colonial Citizenship* (Albany, NY: State University of New York Press, 2010).

4.   Jonathan Clark, *Our Shadowed Present: Modernism, Postmodernism, and History.* (Stanford: Stanford University Press 2004), p. 257.

5. Gabriel Josipovici, *What Ever Happened to Modernism?* (New Haven: Yale University Press 2010), p. 178.

6. Ibid., p. 186.

7. Ibid., p. 187.

8. Dipesh Chakrabarty, "The Muddle of Modernity," *American Historical Review* 116 (June 2011): pp. 663–675, here p. 674.

9. Richard Wolin, "'Modernity': The Peregrinations of a Contested Historiographical Concept," *American Historical Review* 116 (June 2011): pp. 741–751, here, p. 743.

10. Ibid., p. 750.

11. Gabrielle Spiegel, "The Task of the Historian," *American Historical Review* 114 (February 2009): pp. 1–15, here p. 15.

Chapter *10*

The Future of History

The previous chapters of this book opened with a running narrative about a missing roommate. This narrative was linear, rational, and historicist. It moved from a beginning to a middle and then to an end in pursuit of logical explanations from the perspective of the person whose roommate had disappeared. Some internal tensions and confusion were evident, but there was little ambivalence and no irrational babbling such as one might expect of a schizophrenic's account of the past. Most authors employ a rational narrative voice that tells a story along a chronological unfolding of events. In recent decades it has been more fashionable to be creative with chronology. For instance, Quentin Tarantino's film *Pulp Fiction* opens with an episode from the end of the story and then shifts to a chronological unfolding in order to provide context for the ending. In the opening scene, we hear Jules, who is off-screen, talking to Vince as Vince heads to the bathroom. On the opposite side of the restaurant a young couple is enjoying a romantic breakfast. The couple suddenly decides to rob all patrons of the restaurant. By the time the movie viewers return to the opening scene, they know Jules and Vince in a completely different way than they had at the opening. *Pulp Fiction* is a good example of how context changes the way that one understands events. All stories have some form of beginning, middle, and end. Where one places those parts and the order in which one allows the story to unfold will result in quite different accounts of what happened.

Any narrative of reality involves fictionalization of the subject because the writing of narrative turns people and events into figures similar to those found in other narrative accounts. The historian's representation of a real historical person is not the same thing as the real historical person. Even a representation built on extensive primary source analysis is trapped in the tropes of historical narration. The intentions of the text, not the intentions of the writer, thus become central to postmodern historians.

After opening with a narrative story, each chapter of this book turned to a toolbox approach to a wide range of historians. The book does not explicitly champion any one historian or even style of writing, but the actual writing of the book suggests that this is the best way to provide a history of this material for the intended audience. This structuring of the book fits the writing of history at a certain time and in a certain culture. Cultural biases are evident in the way that one structures any book. The table of contents of this book is fairly consistent with traditional English language history books. This table of contents would probably appear long and detailed to Italian readers but short and inadequate to German readers. Textual traditions vary widely from culture to culture. The diversity of textual traditions is not simply a matter of economic or political factors. Cultural factors may be more significant in influencing the packaging of knowledge than basic material conditions.

Just as a table of contents fits cultural expectations, so too archives are the products of cultural, political, and economic decisions. The act of gathering and preserving some information while excluding other information is part of the task of any archivist. Sources that are collected and preserved in a national archive are likely to differ from material collected in other archives. The very act of collecting for a specific archive may taint the validity of the sources. The rise of digital resources has accentuated the importance of evaluating archival bias as historians now have an overabundance of possible sources that were collected for radically different reasons. As such, historians need to be more aware of potential bias. Historians with scarce primary sources may be able to analyze the sources with little consideration of how and why those sources are extant. Historians with abundant data need to explain how and why the sources were chosen from the pool of available sources as well as how and why the pool of available sources was collected and preserved.

The missing roommate spoke to us only through remnants, fragments, and the memory of the narrator. Cultural differences and archival accuracy were not important factors because the roommate and the narrator shared the same historical experiences. For historians, the issues related to cultural differences and archival accuracy are compounded by the fact that the past is different from the present. Few historians still embrace the notion of "the past as a foreign country" in light of the baggage that comes with that phrase: the foreign country entails both a nationalism that will only resonate with some people at certain times in history and a notion of foreignness that exaggerates the homogeneity of a country. Ethnic identities are frequently stronger than national identities and thus foreign might imply other citizens of the same country who speak a different language or have different ethnic traditions. "The otherness of the past" may be preferable to "the past as a foreign country," but the very use of "the other" suggests that the writing is not just about the past. Any imposition of the other suggests that something is other to something else. The other is understood as different from the self or a definable notion of a collective self (such as the imagined community of a nation). If the self is only possible through recognition of the other, then one might surmise that the other is only possible through the recognition of the self. The otherness of the past is an "other" relative to our existence in the present. The past is valuable not because it is different from the present, but because the difference offers something for us in the present.

Most readers will agree that modern life is sufficiently complicated that simplistic explanations are misleading. When explaining the past we may want to make it rational, logical, and simple, but there is no reason to believe that the past is less complicated than the present. Diligent and focused study may make the past more comprehensible, but it may also oversimplify to such an extent that we have a false security about the past. Oversimplification makes the past more comprehensible to students, but it may also render an inaccurate past.

Historians have at their disposal a wide range of plausible methods to construct a story of the past. Meanings will vary contingent on the development of a plot and the overall configuration of a story. Historians need to be conscious of the extent to which their own narrative strategies influence their depictions of the past. The study of historiography affords historians the opportunity to proceed in a more self-critical fashion because the historian is aware of a wider variety of possible representations. The self-critical process of writing may or may not produce a better history, but an awareness of historiography should allow historians to avoid repeating mistakes.

History at its best acknowledges the contemporary process of innovation, renewal, and fermentation in the historical profession without appeal to some lost "golden age" from which history has fallen. The newest historical practices offer exciting possibilities as well as new challenges. Perhaps the greatest challenge involves adapting to changing technology. The education of historians and basic standards of professional conduct have evolved slowly over time, but the new vistas offered by technology have forced professional historians to reevaluate the role of technology in the research, publication, and teaching of history. Digital history, and the digital humanities in general, is here to stay. The question is not whether professional historians will embrace digital history, but how they will embrace it.

10.1 HISTORY AT ITS BEST?

Any attempt to present history at its best will bring harsh cries from a wide range of contemporary scholars and curious reflections from future historians. This book has championed histories that combined a comparative scope, methodological rigor, historicist pursuit of the past's otherness, and awareness of implications for the present. Europeans since Herodotus have employed cultural comparisons as a way of measuring themselves and thus have contributed to Western intellectual values that are difficult to imagine without comparison to a native or less-developed other. Combine this tradition with recent historians' tendency to posit the otherness of the past and the postcolonial championing of the marginal, the hybrid, and otherness that is decidedly non-Western, and the result is a radical rethinking of the self relative to contemporaneous and historical otherness. The postcolonial perspective thus changes the scope of comparative analysis beyond that defined by historians at the end of World War II.

Marc Bloch championed comparative history to combat nationalistic history, and while nationalism is not dead, the newer issue facing historians is that of ethnicity or the familiar versus the strange, the distant versus the close. Comparative encounters combat the hierarchical tendencies that privilege European societies over other peoples. But this purpose is frequently accomplished by privileging both sides of the comparison without consideration of a nonhierarchical analysis that emphasizes the space between the comparative models.

Homi Bhabha's analysis of hybridity revealed that the English discourse incorporated the Indian, and the Indian discourse incorporated the English, thereby creating a third space between the English and Indian. Analysis of this third space avoids such pitfalls as (1) false universals, (2) ethnocentricity, and (3) evolutionary theories of development. One way to facilitate this process is to emphasize and objectify time by exploring contemporaneity that does not place one before or above the other. The pursuit of symmetrical comparative analysis that recognizes parallel goals, rather than positing one as first or better, allows for symmetrical comparison in a frame of contemporaneity that avoids notions of primitives working to catch up.

Comparative history also requires local studies that lend themselves to comparisons that are meaningful to a wider audience. Frequently this moral component leads to teleological notions of progress. Joyce Appleby, past president of the American Historical Association, goes so far in championing moral history as to argue that history "can help human beings think better, live more richly, and act more wisely."[1] The "richness" of life is difficult to ascertain, but certainly thinking better and acting more wisely are laudable goals. Appleby makes no claims of teleological development, but her line of argument runs the risk of reinserting a teleology of improvement, whereby societies think better and act more wisely as the understanding of history expands, unless we restate this function. Namely, humans think less well and do not act as wisely if they lack an understanding of history. The pursuit of history does not necessarily lead humans to evolve into ever better thinking, and more wisely acting, beings, but the absence of historical understanding limits the range of thinking and acting.

10.2   HISTORIANS AND THEIR EDUCATION

Historical curiosity is frequently an exploration of collective strategies by which societies organize and make sense of their experience. Historians thus contribute to the collective management of existential anxiety by constructing historical explanations. Or is the opposite true? Perhaps Voltaire was correct when he had Candide conclude that we should simply tend our gardens. Existential anxiety may be better squelched by tending our gardens than by creating new myths and explanations. History and the pursuit of social truths may create, rather than erase, existential anxiety. Nevertheless, historical curiosity exists in some humans, and it appears to be aroused by a range of incidents such as the disappearance of a roommate. The pursuit of history fosters revisions because new questions drive researchers to rethink the past. Students of history need to understand how historians act and what the contemporary pursuit of history entails in order to benefit from history.

Who are these historians, and what makes them pursue historical curiosity? Two broad and contradicting theories explain the profession as either a civic discipline that is open to all or an autonomous community of specialists. The first option reduces history to things that anyone can readily know and thus denies any claim of originality. Historians become guarantors of factual accuracy instead of interpreters of historical remnants. The second option runs the risk of making historians' discussions irrelevant to anyone beyond the autonomous community of historians. History at its best lies somewhere between these extremes, when it addresses a broad audience without sacrificing standards. Historians need to engage in the development of theoretical and methodological practices related to new fields such as postcolonialism and microhistory in order to foster innovation and avoid obsolescence.

Political and intellectual historians since World War II have reconsidered European values and the way that Europeans have defined themselves. Moreover, the contemporaneous decline of colonial empires, the end of official segregation in the United States, and the increased diversity in academia have contributed to a radically different makeup of professional historians. This change is significant because historical revisionism only succeeds when a consensus of historians accepts the revisions.

The combination of new methodologies, new boundaries of historical inquiry, and a changing demographics of professional historians has contributed to several recent studies about the education of professional historians. In 2004, the American Historical Association's Committee on Graduate Education published *The Education of Historians for the Twenty-first Century*. The Committee on Graduate Education had been given the charge to "examine and report on the training of the nation's [USA] historians."[2] Despite the purported focus on the "the nation's historians," the actual audience is clearly "the entire historical profession."[3]

In the first such study since 1962, when Cold War ideology heightened public interest in the education of historians, the American Historical Association seems to be looking for evidence that the historical profession is in near disarray:

> That the Committee has discovered so many ways to improve graduate education does not mean that current practices are in utter disarray. Rather, it is an indication of the degree of responsibility that graduate faculties and historians in every professional setting feel toward the next generation of historians.[4]

The book is more than a recommendation about graduate education; it serves inadvertently as a model for how history should, or should not, be written. The authors place history on the border between the humanities and social sciences. They employ a survey "intended to elicit vital data" but also "aimed to capture the voices of the directors of graduate studies who are key figures in the practical operation of graduate programs in history."[5] The committee uses data to prove near disarray that can be remedied with "data collection and dissemination" that is "labor intensive."[6] The emphasis on "data" clearly outweighs other voices just as diachronic analysis outweighs synchronic analysis in the book. The authors of this book do not seem to have been influenced by recent methodological innovations in the writing of history. They are interested neither in theory nor creative methodology. As an example of how to write history, the volume is closer to the social sciences of the 1960s than the humanities of the twenty-first century.

10.3 STANDARDS AND PROFESSIONAL CONDUCT

In March 2002, Lynn Hunt, the then current president of the American Historical Association, entitled her "From the President" column of the association's newsmagazine: "Where Have All the Theories Gone?" After stating that "in fact, *theory* has declined everywhere in the humanities," she asks whether the profession has moved "from the Age of Paradigms to the Age of Plagiarism."[7] Public discussions of plagiarism (using the work of other scholars without explaining the source) and professional standards have become fashionable in the twenty-first century because a number of highly visible and distinguished historians were accused of plagiarism and falsifying historical evidence. Some of the accused were professional historians and others were popular author-historians. Some used the work of others without proper attribution of the source and others simply fabricated data that strengthened their argument. It is unclear whether ideological zeal, greedy self-promotion, simple sloppiness, or some combination of factors motivated these cheaters, but cheat they did.

The actions of a small handful of historians created significant repercussions for professional historians around the world. Historians who had long agreed to disagree about objectivity (see Chapter 3) decided that it was time to redefine the boundaries of historical research. The Council of the American Historical Association went so far as to e-mail a copy of its official press release, entitled "AHA Announces Changes in Efforts Relating to Professional Misconduct," to all members of the American Historical Association. The May 7, 2003, press release stated that the council "voted unanimously to develop a series of initiatives aimed at addressing concerns relating to professional conduct. Instead of adjudicating a small number of confidential cases the AHA will mount a major effort to educate historians, their students, and the public about appropriate standards for research and writing as well as employment practices." The AHA decided to end "fifteen years of adjudication because adjudication is not an effective tool for responding to misconduct." Rather than hear cases of misconduct, the "Association will mount a more visible campaign of public education."

The efforts to inform the public included the promotion of a revised *Statement on Standards of Professional Conduct* that "institutions should use when addressing charges of professional misconduct among historians."[8] The *Statement on Standards of Professional Conduct* was first adopted in May of 1987 and has gone through periodic amendments, but the "major revision" currently under way is being made with a hype that was previously absent. Remarkably, there is little new in the 2003 revisions to deal with the plagiarism issues that precipitated the recent hype.

Professional standards do matter, but they are better left to the community of historians debating in open forums such as conferences and refereed journals. Peer review remains the best method to maintain standards. Students are encouraged to read and cite refereed journals and periodicals.

10.4 DIGITAL HISTORY

Benedict Anderson redefined the notions of nationalism and national history in his 1983 book *Imagined Communities: Reflections on the Origin and Spread of Nationalism*. He argued that nations were imagined communities.

It is physically possible to interact with only a limited community that is far smaller in scope than a nation. Thus, a nation is "an imagined political community" because people are only imagining participation with others.[9] The nation, or political community, is imagined as limited (with finite boundaries), as sovereign, and as a community (with a sense of fraternity). Technological innovations in printing and the rise of capitalism contributed to the rise of the notion of nationalism. Anderson argues that print capitalists had a vested interest in publishing things in vernacular languages. This fostered the creation of territorialized communities that shared a language. Latin Christendom lost its grip on individuals when "the convergence of capitalism and print technology on the fatal diversity of human language created the possibility of a new form of imagined community, which in its basic morphology set the stage for the modern nation."[10] Anderson rounds out the argument by showing how nationalism is intertwined with the notion of internationalism in what he refers to as "nationalism's undivorcible marriage to internationalism."[11] His trinity of print capitalism, vernacularization of languages, and marriage to internationalism created imagined communities of nations that are deeply entrenched in contemporary human identity.

Anderson mentions in the Afterword to the 2006 revised edition of the book that his book would not have made such an international splash (it is available in twenty-nine languages) had it not been written in English and published in London. He modestly attributes the success of the book not to its qualities, but rather to the fact that English has recently taken on the role of global hegemonic that was once held by Latin. So a book about the effects of print capitalism on the vernacularization of languages appeared at the same time that vernacular languages were being destroyed by the Internet's and mass media's emphasis on English as the international language of educated people. This may suggest a shift toward internationalism. Or perhaps the existence of translations into twenty-nine languages suggests that vernacularization and thus the imagined communities of nationalism are far from disappearing.

The recent rise of English as an international language of educated people, the popularity of the internet, and the abundance of digitized books and information have contributed to a shift in how knowledge is communicated. Prior to the digital age, knowledge was based on the materiality of the book. In the twentieth century, scholars devoted an unusual amount of energy to analysis of signs, texts, and linguistic structures of language and material books. Books were living things that contained the original printed text, but also writings, notes, markings, and stains that reflected sections of specific interest or distrust for diverse readers. The Jewish Torah contains scriptures surrounded by the unfolding commentaries as well as commentaries about the commentaries.

Like ivy creeping up the walls of an old building, the material book had a life of its own that was more than the printed words.

Readers can smell, touch, and experience a book and the remnants of its past readers in a manner that currently does not exist for digital publications. An old PDF file is sterile in comparison to an old bound book. Digitization has transposed the aesthetics of printed knowledge. The library as the fixed system of books has been replaced by digital images of texts. This greatly expedites access to material and also destroys the communal experience of previous distribution systems such as libraries and book stores. These venues offered important social opportunities that may not be replaced with the shift to digital commons.

The digitalization of information offers access to texts and data to people around the world. The digital transformation of the field of history has grown from its origins in the 1960s and 1970s when cliometrics and the quantification of data collection changed the scope of historical inquiry. The focus on data collection shifted to data dissemination in the 1980s with the rise of electronic text and early e-mail. The 1990s brought a democratization of knowledge with the internet, online syllabi, and the rise of hypertext (http is short for HyperText Transfer Protocol). The developments that contributed to this democratization of information also contributed to a shift away from chronological analysis toward synchronic analysis. Hypertext creates a nonlinear unfolding of ideas as the online reader clicks from one idea to another in a pattern that is more apt to follow a synchronic (jump from idea to related idea) than a diachronic (examine the chronological unfolding of an idea) presentation of knowledge. In the 2000s, search engines such as Google came to play an important role in how scholars accessed internet information. Google and Google Books furthered the democratization of digital knowledge as scholars around the world shared access to a host of scholarly material. Accessibility was no longer limited as the world's libraries began the shift to one vast open-stack digital collection. Curmudgeons may bemoan the loss of seeking a book on a shelf and serendipitously finding something shelved nearby, but the speed of the web offers new opportunities for serendipitous discovery. Accessibility and interactive aspects of the web have exploded in the 2010s as social media and bloggers allowed organizations and scholars to connect in new ways. The future offers even more promise for the growth of collaborative research and the rise of active learning.

The future is difficult to predict but sentiment in 2013 is for the expansion of GeoHumanities and the three-dimensional depictions of virtual reality that GIS (Geographic Information Systems) offers. The focus on layered geology, referred to as the spatial turn, moves the field of geography from an empirical backdrop to history and replaces it with the notion that geography is an interpretive field of analysis. Cultural geography takes its place with the cross-pollinations discussed in Chapter 4 (cultural anthropology and cultural sociology). The new digital age has moved us far beyond mere digitalization of texts and thus forced historians to become aware of interdisciplinary possibilities.

The interdisciplinary trend of digital history corresponds with a recent inter-institutional trend as digital history shifts from institution-based projects (like the Center for History and New Media at George Mason University or the Virginia Center for Digital History at the University of Virginia) to field-specific projects that tap many institutions such as H-Net (which has a tie to Michigan State University and also to several other institutions) and the World History Association. These venues create technological and epistemological frameworks for scholars to engage historical problems and scholarship.

Perhaps the most important trend is the expansion of experiential and emotive characteristics of digital history. The goal of most digital history projects has been to create an experience whereby the viewer can process something rather than to have a thesis or product that the viewer will know. Scholarship and rational analysis are not abandoned, but they are molded into an experience that appeals to more than cerebral logic. Consumers of digital media may test various possibilities instead of being led to a specific conclusion. This gives participants a sense of ownership in the results that does not traditionally exist with the reader of a print monograph. This focus on the process of understanding the past will appeal to a wider audience than traditional print texts.

Three examples of early digital history projects that have focused on process over product are (1) *The Valley of the Shadow*, by the Virginia Center for Digital History at the University of Virginia; (2) *Imagining the French Revolution: Depictions of the French Revolutionary Crowd*, a project done for the American Historical Association by the Roy Rosenzweig Center for History and New Media, George Mason University and the Department of History, University of California, Los Angeles; and (3) *The Texas Slavery Project*, by the Virginia Center for Digital History at the University of Virginia. All three projects include guidance for teachers who might use the sites in the classroom. *The Valley of the Shadow* project consists of digital archives for people living in Augusta County, Virginia and Franklin County, Pennsylvania during the era of the Civil War. The archive of primary source texts is supplemented with some maps and images. Of the three projects it is the closest to an archive and does not contain scholarly summary. *Imagining the French Revolution* consists of forty-two images of crowds in the French Revolution along with essays and an online discussion by seven scholars. The work allows students to view the images and explore how scholars have interpreted them.

The site shows how scholars use images and how they disagree over interpretations, but the focus is really on the scholarly product and the essays, and not on providing tools for students to use in a classroom discussion or written text. *The Texas Slavery Project* is a database of population information from 1837 to 1845 for counties in what is now the state of Texas. It also includes statistical estimates for any missing data. The data are combined with maps in a manner that traces the expansion of slavery in the American Southwest. The interactive maps allow viewers to see patterns of slavery changing over time. Overall, the site offers more direction than the *Valley of the Shadow* and more primary source material than *Imagining the French Revolution*. These digital projects move the field of digital history well beyond the mere digitalization of texts. The shift in focus from product to process also offers wonderful opportunities for scholarship and teaching.

The improved accessibility and democratization of information will undoubtedly foster more collaborative projects in the future. The increase in bloggers and the growing presence of professional subfield organizations on the internet will allow historians to test ideas and alter research at a quicker pace than ever before. This means that historians will need to be more flexible in contemplating diverse ideas. It also means that they will need to be better versed in theory and methodologies beyond their own subfields in order to distinguish between solid and shoddy material.

Methodological and historiographical issues come to the forefront in the evaluation of solid digital scholarship. Refereed publications take on a new role as professional standards are established for digital publications. In February of 2012, the American Historical Association issued a call for submissions for the *AHR Prize in Digital Historical Scholarship* along with six criteria: (1) "original interpretation of historical evidence" or "original theoretical or methodological approach to the interpretation of the past"; (2) "the *digital* tools and modalities must contribute substantially to the argument" (modalities are defined to include interactivity, multimodality, and database and network connectivity); (3) "scope and scale . . . must approximate . . . the *short form* of historical argumentation" (6,000–8,000 words of standard text exclusive of citations); (4) "the textual argumentation of the work can be structured in nonlinear, interactive ways . . . but the argument . . . must be clearly visible and identifiable"; (5) "the argumentative text must be supported by citations to archival sources and to relevant secondary scholarship"; and (6) "all archival objects presented in the work . . . must be fully captioned and cited."[12] The American Historical Association clearly wants to insure the trustworthiness of the scholarship while opening new vistas for the technical and epistemological structures of digital production.

   Digital history will influence the profession in myriad ways due to the tendency toward synchronic history, the expanded accessibility, the focus on learning as process instead of product, the encouragement of interdisciplinary collaboration, and the rise of new methodological issues. Perhaps the greatest reason for professional historians to engage digital history is that the failure to do so may have harmful consequences for history if the field of digital history comes to be defined by online participants who lack a fundamental understanding of historiography and historical methodology.

10.5 CONCLUSION

Some historians believe that the profession is in an era of crisis because of the dramatic transformations brought about by the changing makeup of professional historians and the new theoretical and methodological practices described in this book. But history is not in crisis. The innovative methods and focuses will allow historians to avoid the crisis of stagnancy and to create meaningful memories for the future. Previously mute people have been turned into historical actors and authors. Exotic cultures and differences are no longer regarded as expressions of backwardness. Instead, the historical actor is now understood within a complex web of local cultural understandings that have implications that are not purely local.

   History in Crisis? is a conscious rejection of a critical tradition that grandly proclaims "crisis" so the critic can then explain the world. The absence of "crisis" makes the positing of a solution more difficult and runs the risk of offering little new. I have examined facets of individual historians' works in pursuit of broad tendencies and trends. No attempt has been made to master great historians by systematically analyzing the evolution of their thought. My goal has not been to proclaim the novelty of recent historians so that they may be assimilated, via some Wilsonian paradigm, into manageable and masterable subjects. Instead of proclaiming masters who are then mastered, I have sought to provide a toolbox or workshop so that readers can get hands-on experience analyzing and evaluating a vast range of historical writing.

   Reading *History in Crisis?* is not a substitute for reading historical monographs and articles. To the contrary, it should challenge you to read a variety of historical explanations. Moreover, it has avoided the tendency to champion new masters because we can also learn how not to write history from poor exemplars. The secret is to take the toolbox and begin to read histories written by diverse historians.

Readers of a wide range of historical methodologies are encouraged to consider the six reasons to study history presented in Chapter 1 of this book: (1) history cures us of provincialism by showing that change is the only constant, (2) history is to time what anthropology is to space in that differences occur over time, (3) the otherness of the past is a product of these changes over time, (4) the historical perspective of this otherness cures us of our provincialism by revealing the uncanniness of our own world, (5) this memory of the past is necessary because our collective memory defines us, and (6) therefore we need ambitious and passionate historians who are willing to create new questions and answers. The pursuit of new questions and new histories should prevent history as a field of study from becoming stagnant. The dynamic craft of history is enhanced by the new varieties of historical representation.

The plethora of historical methodologies and the ability to avoid some quest for a holy grail of universalizing social theory actually contribute to the vibrancy of historical pursuit. Contrary to conventional wisdom, history is not in crisis: postmodernism, postcolonialism, and the rise in literary criticism of self-defined New Historicists all contribute to a new type of history and a new role for history. Postmodernism reveals the fallacies of the literary form that historians have embraced without questioning for thousands of years. Moreover, the rejection of the very possibility of universal standards means that standards are historically contingent. Kuhn's theory of paradigms in science is superseded by the notion that all knowledge is merely linguistic convention. History offers the best opportunity for exploring the factors that created the expressions, the range of recipients' receptions, and the general contingency of knowledge. Knowledge exists within a historical context, so history subsumes all other disciplines: the Archimedean point for evaluating the respective merits of any form of discourse becomes a historical problem. Recent developments in theory do not signal an end to the pursuit of truths; they instead require analysis of the historical contingency of those truths.[13]

Readers of this book have received a brief overview of recent historiography. The goal was to provide a theoretical toolbox instead of a litany of acceptable practices. Theoretical issues, such as what is objectivity, have been discussed with no mention of how to read a historical source objectively. As evidenced by recent publications of the American Historical Association, questions of sources and professional conduct are an important part of the profession that are worthy of exploration. On the other hand, too strong of a focus on professional standards may well stifle creativity and historical imagination. Students interested in how to use a primary source are encouraged to read the extensive literature on the actual writing of history.[14]

The current historical conversation is vastly wider than the historical conversation that existed fifty years ago. The new conversation will remain vibrant as long as historians continue to blur the boundaries of history by incorporating methodological innovations, novel theories, and new voices into the writing of history. Readers of this book are encouraged to join the currently expanding historical conversation. Let the conversation continue!

NOTES

1. Joyce Appleby, "The Power of History," *American Historical Review* 103 (February 1998): 1 14, here p. 1.

2. Thomas Bender, Philip M. Katz, Colin Palmer, and the AHA Committee on Graduate Education, *The Education of Historians for the Twenty-first Century* (Urbana, IL: University of Illinois Press, 2004), p. xiii.

3. Ibid., p. xv.

4. Ibid., p. 85.

5. Ibid., p. xv.

6. Ibid., p. 86.

7. Lynn Hunt, "Where Have All the Theories Gone?" *Perspectives: Newsmagazine of the American Historical Association* 40 (March 2002): 5–7, here p. 5.

8. American Historical Association, *Statement on Standards of Professional Conduct* (Washington, DC: American Historical Association, 2003).

9. Benedict Anderson, *Imagined Communities: Reflections on the Origin and Spread of Nationalism* revised edition (New York: Verso, 2006), pp. 5–6.

10. Ibid., p. 46.

11. Ibid., p. 207.

12. "Call for Submissions for the AHR Prize for the Best Digital Article *Perspectives: Newsmagazine of the American Historical Association* 50 (February 2012) pp. 12–13.

13. For more on the hope that the study of history provides see Ernst Breisach, *On the Future of History: The Postmodernist Challenge and Its Aftermath* (Chicago: University of Chicago Press, 2003). Breisach maintains that "the record of the human experience" is "always incompletely understood but cumulatively becoming clearer" (p. 208).

14. Robert C. Williams has written a student-friendly introduction to the actual writing of history entitled, *The Historian's Toolbox: A Student's Guide to the Theory and Craft of History* (Armonk, NY: M.E. Sharpe, 2011).

Index